The pandemic has been a global limit experience that has deeply impacted humanity. *Who Are We After the Pandemic?* is a question that this wonderful book invites us to reflect on, a book that analyses the complexity of what happened to us as individuals and as humanity. From a humanistic perspective, this essay helps us explore essential life dimensions such as work, education, the relationship with the world and nature, and love. It is not only a theoretical reflection, but also a rich experiential text that gives examples of different people's lives in which we can see ourselves reflected and reconnect with experiences we lived. The book helps to consider the impact of virtuality and technology, that, on the one hand, invited us to create new scenarios and, on the other, generated inauthentic experiences, loneliness, addiction, estrangement, disorganization, and lack of corporeality. Can there be experience without a body? The erotic-emotional bonds, the virtualization of love and intimacy, is another of the issues analysed. With no doubt, reading this book helps us to become aware of the complexity of the phenomenon that humanity has experienced. The authors integrate a humanistic perspective that sheds light on the possibility of recovering an authentic encounter with ourselves and within our bonds.

Héctor Fernández Álvarez, PhD in Psychology. Founder and Honorary President of Fundación Aiglé. Creator of the Integrative-Cognitive Psychotherapeutic Model of Fundación Aiglé. Author of different books and articles on Mental Health and Integrative Psychotherapy

Durao and Segafredo's work bravely uncovers the breadth and depth of how humans at the limit have used untested technology both to create and to dehumanize. The writing itself, with its moving clinical examples and massive collection of existentialist wisdom, exemplifies with warmth and complexity the humanness it aims to promote.

Jeffery Smith, MD, DLFAPA
Associate Clinical Professor of Psychiatry, New York Medical College
Leader of the Psychotherapy Caucus of the American Psychiatric Association

Conjuring Karl Jaspers' wisdom that who we are, and who we are together, are disclosed when we are thrown into foundering by boundary or limit situations, Marian Durao and Gaspar Segafredo deepen this most necessary of existential confrontations with exquisite care in their new book, *Who Are We After the Pandemic? Psychology, Technology and Relationships*. They arrive on the scene with this text like existential first responders helping us rummage through the debris in the havoc wreaked by the recent pandemic for ourselves and each other. Through each chapter they walk with us as we search for remnants of our shattered identities and communities amidst our ongoing mistrust of life's instability and betrayal. Yet, Durao and Segafredo are indeed agents of hope and help spotlight our way out of this bewilderment as we whistle through dangerous times, knowing all along we can't return home. When lonely and in tears, or not only wondering *who we are* after the pandemic, but also *are we at all* after the pandemic, reach for this book as a friend. It will guide you, and us, to our new home of living and trusting once again. Bravo!

Todd Dubose, PhD
Professor, The Chicago School of Professional Psychology,
Past President of APA's Division 32 (The Society for Humanistic Psychology)

An existential, integrative, and open perspective is the proposal that Durao and Segafredo develop in this exciting book. Technology and relationships are two inseparable realities from the vicissitudes of contemporary living in which the authors immerse us hand in hand with outstanding thinkers who converge to illuminate the cases they present. The search for new bonds through technology that brings greater loneliness and emptiness became more visible and intense when we've been thrown into this "odyssey, where the oceans of the physical and the virtual presence intersect, hiding existential riches to be discovered and created, but also a kind of Matrix, just waiting for us to slip up," as the authors point out. *Who Are We After the Pandemic* is undoubtedly essential reading to understand ourselves better, when our existences approach the edges of life.

Ramiro Gómez Salas, PhD in Psychology
President of the Peruvian Association of Phenomenological-Existential Psychology

Who Are We After the Pandemic? Each reflective human being should ask this question, but few actually do. Many seem to brush this question under the carpet, pretending nothing serious happened. But we did encounter a collective boundary situation in human history, a transition to what some have described as a 'new normal.' But what is normal? What do we want this new normal to be? Studies across the globe suggest that during and after the pandemic, most individuals have asked some existential questions about themselves, others, and the world. The lack of answers to their existential questions seemed to go hand in hand with existential anxiety and psychopathology. Thus, we cannot leave these existential questions unanswered, as this would impinge our well-being as well as limit our potential to learn from this crisis. Marian Durao and Gaspar Segafredo undertake this crucial task to examine who we are, who we can be, and who we may want to be. They were right to delve into the inspiring body of existential literature on how humans can cope with an existential crisis. They remind us of the human potential of creativity, meaning, and connectedness—crucial in an era in which we may feel narrowed down by a medical/epidemiological gaze, technology, and social isolation. They show resources to relate in a more free and human way to the reductionistic technological systems in which we live—what the existential philosopher Martin Heidegger has described as a key topic for our era. Ultimately, Durao's and Segafredo's ask a question to us: How will we live our daily life, and how will we contribute to the macrocosm of the community and planet? Who are you, and who do you want to be?

Joel Vos, PhD, MSc, MA, CPsychol, FHEA, Senior Researcher and Senior Lecturer at the Metanoia Institute, London (UK), Director of IMEC International Meaning Events and Community. Author of *Psychology of COVID-19*, *The Economics of Meaning in Life*, and *Meaning in Life: An Evidence-Based Handbook for Practitioners*

What I like the most about *Who Are We After the Pandemic* by Durao and Segafredo is that it does not try to be eclectic by reconciling theories but rather integrates them harmoniously, resulting in a profound work that is didactic and informative while being enjoyable. Starting from the idea of human as a biopsychosocial-spiritual being inextricably linked to one's sociocultural context, the authors highlight the importance of corporality as a condition for the insertion of being in the world and of the redefinition of this world crossed by the virtuality brought by the pandemic. This work describes with fluid language this global situation that came to put interpersonal relationships in check, especially the therapeutic relationship. In this sense, the inclusion of clinical cases in the book is extremely illuminating. In short, it is a highly recommended book not only for health professionals, but also for the curious reader who is concerned about the changes we are going through.

Marta B. Guberman, PhD in Psychology, Specialist in Clinical Psychology and Psychodiagnosis, Professor at National and Latin American Universities, Founding member of the Argentine Logotherapy Foundation and the Latin American Association of Existential Psychotherapy (ALPE).

Who Are We After the Pandemic?

Psychology, Technology, and Relationships

By Marian Durao and Gaspar Segafredo

(Translation by Claudia Pesce)

University
PROFESSORS PRESS

Colorado Springs, CO
www.universityprofessorspress.com

Published in 2023, University Professors Press.

Paperback ISBN: 978-1-955737-16-6
ebook ISBN: 978-1-955737-17-3

University Professors Press
Colorado Springs, CO
www.universityprofessorspress.com

Cover Design by Laura Ross
Cover Art by Marguerite Laing

Table of Contents

Acknowledgments

Marian Durao

I would like to thank my father, who instilled in me a passion for knowledge; my children, for awakening in me an early interest in technology; and my family in general, who accompany me at every step and are the fundamental pillar of my life. Gaspar, my co-author, thank you for making this time of global pandemic an experience of shared reflection and emotional support.

I would like to thank my mentors Héctor Fernández-Álvares, Diana Kirszman, Hugo Hirsch and Elena Scherb who have helped me to develop my global perspective within the field of psychotherapy. Thanks to Dr. Kirk Schneider for his kind words. I would especially like to thank my patients, with whom I have worked at a distance and who have let me accompany them in their COVID-19 hospitalizations, as well as in their daily lives, in times of fear and uncertainty.

Gaspar Segafredo

First of all, I would like to thank Marian for inviting me to join her in this adventure. Many thanks to my two teachers in this wonderful and challenging profession of psychotherapy: Marta Ester González, for her social and emotional commitment; and Marta Guberman, for her spontaneous and concrete existential view. Also my thanks to other therapists who in different ways have shared their teachings with me: Ona Albornoz, Gabriel Castellá, Beatriz Gómez, Yaqui Martínez Robles, Martín Reynoso, Kirk Schneider, Susana Signorelli, and Adriana Sosa Terradas. I would also like to thank my patients, who have allowed me to accompany them on a part of their journey.

Special thanks to my partner Marisol Alonso, for her love and attentive insights; to my parents, Dorina and Francesco, and to my sisters, Agata and Ariadna, who have read fragments during the writing process and know the background for some of the reflections that date back to the beginning; to my sons, Lorenzo and Leonardo, who teach me every day the depth and meaning of emotional bonds.

Foreword

Kirk J. Schneider

Who Are We After the Pandemic is a beautiful meditation, thoroughly researched and exquisitely worded, on both the perils and promise of technological innovation in the face of COVID-19. Marian Durao and Gaspar Segafredo weave a lucid and compelling case for the resurgence of an existential sensibility at a time when the seduction of high tech has only accelerated. The Covid 19 crisis has not only reinforced our pursuit of the speed, instant results, and appearance and packaging that have marked our contemporary lifestyles, it has profoundly imperiled our capacity for presence and the living, breathing excitement of person-to-person relationships.

We speak much of living in "existential times" these days, but existential concepts go far beyond the question of survival. This book shows acutely that existential inquiry and practice have always been relevant to the human condition but have become especially so in the context of the pandemic. For today we are faced with the existential implications not only of survival—of life and death—but of *how to live, what deeply matters to us*, as the COVID-19 crisis has sharpened the urgency of such challenges. The authors carefully unpack these questions with a series of finely tuned discussions about the problems arising from the pandemic, such as social isolation, stressful uncertainty, notable changes in lifestyle and work habits, and most eloquently, our increasing resorting to high tech devices such as our computers and smartphones. The authors raise intimate questions about this situation, such as: What does it really mean to forgo "live" conversations with each other? How do we relate to each other with less physical contact? What does it mean to continually worry about contagion both from ourselves and through contact with others? And how can we find acceptance, meaning, creativity, and fulfilling encounters in the face of such difficulties? The authors use relatable, everyday case illustrations to vivify their inquiries.

But Durao and Segafredo don't stop there. They perceptively adopt the wide-angle lens and turn our attention to the sociopolitical dimensions of the crisis. These dimensions include our susceptibility to not only admiring or even emulating the machine model for living, but to actually becoming machines—as I have warned in my book *The Spirituality of Awe: Challenges to the Robotic Revolution*. In this context, the authors clearly articulate the nightmare corporate vision (as set forth in films like *The Matrix*). Namely, they describe the way people can be manipulated into perfect consuming machines, such that each button that they push not only gratifies their own quick fix/instant results fantasies but pours shovelfuls of cash into the coffers of advertisers, manufacturers, and owners of the technocratic–militarized complex.

The authors then draw on the bountiful literature of existential–humanistic psychology to address or at least help optimize our response to these thorny scenarios. For example, they point powerfully to the ironic possibility that the pandemic and all our reliance on immortality-promoting machinery could implode into a renewed appreciation for mortality, the flesh-and-blood allure of our bodies, and the preciousness of the transient nature of life. They note the philosopher Martin Buber's profound distinction between "I–It" relations and "I–Thou" relations, which comes into much more acute focus now. Is it possible, they intimate, that the pandemic with all its restrictions and reminders of life's fragility could actually accentuate our desire to relate to one another in our fuller humanity; that it could actually optimize our capacity to live as separate but related beings who recognize the vitality of an interconnected (I–Thou) world?

In the end, the authors raise more questions than they answer—which is appropriate in this bedazzling arena of self and not self, being and simulacrum. That said, this is a masterful inquiry in both scope and biopsychosocial depth. This work is the most substantive integration of psychology, technology, and the challenge of human bonding of which I am aware. The authors are to be congratulated for their diligence, their attention to detail and case examples, and their knowledge of the extant research literature, all of which can help guide us toward a more humane future. The question of what it means to be fully, experientially human and how that understanding pertains to the vital and fulfilled life is arguably the core issue of our time, and this book will be a milestone in the effort to address it.

Introduction

Shall we seize the courage necessary to preserve our sensitivity, awareness and responsibility in the face of radical change? We are called upon to do something new, to confront a no man's land, to push into a forest where there are no well-worn paths and from which no one has returned to guide us. ~ Rollo May

Since 2020, which will be remembered as the year of the COVID-19 pandemic, our relationship with the world, with others, and with ourselves has changed.

Will we ever return to pre-pandemic "normality"? Two and a half millennia ago, Heraclitus understood that no one ever steps in the same river twice: Its waters are always flowing, and it's not the same river. The historic disruption caused by the pandemic may be seen as a deluge that widened the normal flow of existence. In the depths of these waters, there are different intertwined aspects, which we will analyze from a psychological perspective that can't be separated from the social one. On the one hand, we have the disruption of our contemporary way of life and its apparent certainty, witnessed as a global and synchronous crisis of humanity and of each person who is a part of it, a clear manifestation of how the collective and the individual are shaped, contained, and reflected. On the other hand, we have the vertiginous technologization and virtualization of love, education, work, and so many other areas of life. At that intersection of crisis and virtualization, we find that our subjective discomfort has taken certain alienating forms, as well as an appeal to deploy our existential faculties as a possible response.

The problems, the solutions attempted, and the questions that arise on a daily basis have significant relational and technological dimensions, with an inexorable existential background. All this is rooted in processes that already occurred before the pandemic but were accelerated and multiplied by this historic circumstance, which also summons the humanist sensitivity present in each one of us.

Quarantines and social distancing have brought the paradoxes that characterize this era and will likely continue to do so for several years to come. We've experienced physical isolation from others, as well as an extreme and constant technological connection with them. These are two polar opposites: the distance between friends, family members, and even partners, and the sudden constant coexistence with some of them. There is an isolation from our loved ones, as well as the possibility that this absence may awaken in us the appreciation of relationships that we took for granted.

In this framework of relational paradoxes, we have an almost complete irruption of technology in our lives, as a necessary mediatization that has partly compensated for the isolation. Practically overnight, work and education moved massively into the virtual office and classroom: chats with friends on WhatsApp or video games (in the case of teenagers); birthday parties on Zoom; the attempt to meet people on Tinder and other dating apps (a trend that was already present but which spread even among those who thought they would never use it); even psychotherapy sessions went from the office to the video call. Beyond the readjustment each country has made, with their epidemiological and governmental comings and goings, the virtualization of our lives is here to stay. What does this mean in our existence? Does it simplify and improve it because it saves us hours of driving or riding in public transportation and allows us to be just a click away from the place and the person we need to see? Or does it impoverish it because we are not present in it? What consequences will the constant editing of our conversations and the photoshopping or filtering of our shared photos have on our capacity for dialogue and the ability to appreciate reality? Do the various solidary, altruistic, and bonding initiatives that have been channeled through digital platforms mean this is the beginning of new possibilities? Will we end up becoming instruments ourselves, or will we be able to channel human encounter technologically?

These questions shape the new forms of subjective discomfort, together with the constant and deep uncertainty brought on by the pandemic with its marches and counter-marches, and economic, social, and cultural crises. It is summarized by a break with our contemporary way of being and living. It is, in other words, an existential crisis, which may be understood as a collective and individual (and planetary) limit situation, with its pathological risks and its opportunities to build ways of life that are more coherent with what we value. We believe that this crisis calls for the existential–spiritual faculties that are latent in every human being. These can be summarized as the capacity to be present in the fullest possible way and to accept the reality of life; to find or construct meaning in the different moments of life; to face whatever happens and how we feel (even anguish) with creativity and transformation; to promote genuine human encounter in which we open ourselves up to the other in the sharing of experiences and in the shared experience of the "we."

From the psychological standpoint, we propose four possible trends in relation to the understanding of the current discomfort. We call them trends in the sense that they exceed the boundaries of clinical conditions (which they may also reach) and are manifested and spread with different nuances. The first is the psycho-emotional pandemic of anxiety and depression, which arises from the extreme uncertainty, and which will leave its traces even after the complete vaccination of the population and the possible economic recovery of the countries of the world. The second trend is the degree of narcissism and inauthenticity stimulated by digital society, which permeates our relationship with ourselves. This is linked to the egocentric world to which we are reduced by algorithms and the addiction to popularity in social media, which, in a new paradox, may encourage us to falsify the self and hide the consequent feeling of emptiness. The third trend involves our relationship with the world in the widespread addiction to connection and the difficulty of being present. This not only refers to the problematic consumption of the Internet itself but also to the installation of a culture of permanent, fragmented, and superficial connection with innumerable experiences, which involve not immersing oneself experientially in even one of them. The fourth trend we analyze is that of marginalization and violence in relationships with others, explicitly manifested in the increase of cyberbullying, objectification, and social anxiety.

In several ways, these trends in our contemporary subjective discomfort, which is both individual and social, call upon the use of our existential faculties. Deploying them not only involves the opportunity to alleviate suffering but also to deepen our humanity, linked to our freedom and our relational existence. The virtual world will also require a place in the channeling and potentiation of this process.

The first part of this book corresponds to our conceptual framework, to the anthropological vision, and to the analysis of the pandemic as a limit situation. The second part refers to a practical application of the reflections, both with respect to the current way of life, as well as to the discomfort and the related subjective resources. We have decided on a logical order, where the more theoretical aspect precedes the more concrete applications; however, we believe that the reader may choose other paths, which are also valid. Likewise, the interdependence of the two parts and the four chapters does not preclude their internal autonomy.

Faced with the questions raised by this historic turning point, we are testing possible horizons and paths, aware that change continues on a daily basis and that there are no closed answers. We are in uncharted territory. Our exploration has an integrative and humanistic compass and outlines its cartographies in interaction with clinical experience;[1] empirical research; psychological, philosophical, and sociological authors; and, inexorably, with our personal experiences of the pandemic. If the initial maps drawn up with these ideas help contribute to the reader's own explorations, and even to an expansion of new cartographies and landscapes in the field, they will have served their purpose.

---

[1] The cases described in this essay are based on real cases, but some information has been modified in several aspects, even cross-referenced, so that there is no way that the identities and stories of their real protagonists can be recognized. Therefore, these are not intended to be detailed clinical presentations of therapeutic processes, but rather exemplifications that bring to life and inspire the reflections presented here.

Part 1

Humanity and the Person in Crisis

Chapter 1

Being Human Today

A Vision of the Human Being

There is a vision of the human being at the core of any scientific, philosophical, artistic, and even everyday perspective. Whether it is more or less explicit, the concept of person and humanity not only constructs thought but also motivations and expectations and, ultimately, the way we relate to the world, to others, and to ourselves. In the specific field of clinical psychology, for example, it will completely define the therapeutic approach, its possibilities, and limitations. The assistance and intervention of a therapist who considers that a person is driven mainly by instinct will be quite different from another therapist who sees social adaptation as the driving force, and both will contrast with a third who considers that the search for meaning is the fundamental human motivation. The anthropological vision is the foundation of the theory of mind (or psyche), of change, and of human pathology (and, we may add, of potentiality) that sustains each psychotherapeutic perspective.

The vision of person and humanity that inspires and sustains this essay is integrative and humanistic. It is integrative in terms of the consideration of the inseparable multidimensionality that shapes the person as a bio-psychosocial-spiritual being in context (relational and environmental), and of subjectivity as an open totality whose physiological and neurological, emotional and cognitive, relational, and even existential and spiritual aspects are in constant interaction and interdependence. It is humanistic in the sense that it recognizes in each person their leading role in the construction of their own existence, that of others, and of humanity itself. It also views the potential each individual has to expand and develop the awareness of self and of the relational existence that defines us, even to the point of achieving a planetary consciousness. This is based on several humanistic, psychological, and philosophical perspectives, linked to existentialism and phenomenology, as well as relational perspectives, full presence, and complex thinking.

Pauline's Experience as a Starting Point

Pauline is infected with COVID at the start of the pandemic, in a foreign country where she has just separated from her partner and where she has almost no relationships. She is 32 years old, very afraid of going through the disease in isolation and dying alone (this is back when the disease was spreading rapidly and there was little knowledge about it). She began her psychotherapy treatment a month and a half before contracting the COVID-19 virus, with the aim of addressing interpersonal problems with her partner at the time as well as dissatisfaction with her socio-emotional and work life. She is a music teacher, but she longs to be a singer and says she is frustrated that she hasn't tried harder. In her first sessions, she reveals the mark left by her parents' divorce on her childhood, which led her to move to another country with her mother. As a result, her mother suffered from depression, which prevented her from being a mother to Pauline in a (sufficiently) supportive way. To sum up, Pauline's distress and the reason she seeks psychotherapeutic help are linked to an emptiness she feels in her relationships, related to an insecure attachment pattern, and in her life. In addition to the emptiness in her relationships and life, there is also the limit situation of being infected by an unknown and potentially fatal disease. This limit situation also takes on a global scale, in a context of collective uncertainty.

As the viral illness progresses, the physical discomfort is accentuated along with her anguish and fears, especially in relation to the absence of loved ones, both due to her social and viral situation. She stays in complete isolation at home; a doctor periodically monitors her physical condition through video calls. The prescription is rest, hydration, and fever medication. She stays in bed for several days, not even having the strength to take a bath and with no desire to eat. The main emotional support is provided by her therapist, who sees her on a daily basis. With the therapist, Pauline expresses her physical pain as well as her emotional and mental suffering, and from time to time asks herself questions about her existence. What are the things and people she truly values in her life? How does she want to live? What is she most committed to in life, and would she change that?

From her particular experience, Pauline represents in a certain way the contemporary pandemic and post-pandemic situation. It is a critical context that disrupts an already unsatisfactory way of life, maintained by the day-to-day inertia and the demand to "perform" productively without being aware of where we are going. This raises questions about existence itself, from the physical, emotional, cognitive, relational, and spiritual multidimensionality of the human being. In line with existentialist humanism, that of full presence and the psychology that draws from these sources, we find in the individual case the traces of common humanity. The experiential richness of Pauline's case, which we will be analyzing at some points of the chapter together with other cases, allows us to elucidate our anthropological vision of a multidimensional being in a state of becoming and in relation, who exercises freedom in the context of finitude, as well as the transforming potential of crises.

Unique, Multidimensional, and in a State of Becoming

Each person is a unique and multidimensional gestalt, in a constant state of becoming. Both Karl Jaspers and Viktor Frankl describe the person as "a bio-psycho-spiritual being living in community" (Oro, 2016, p. 174). The understanding of this being can only be reached in the unique and unrepeatable case of a particular person. To bring that synthesis of existential psychology closer to the widespread conception of "biopsychosocial being" in the field of health, we may go further and state that we speak of a bio-psychosocial-spiritual being. In Pauline, we clearly see how the physical ailment caused by the viral infection interacts and overlaps with her emotional suffering, which is also mounted on her fragile social network and her insecure attachment pattern; this, together with the limit situation, generates a series of existential questions about what she really values in life, about what appeals to her, about meaning. A disruption in one dimension involves and is juxtaposed to the others. Pauline's moment of crisis is expressed in multiple dimensions. Also, her way of being, her subjectivity, and her bond with otherness are defined by the particular interaction and bio-psychosocial-spiritual overlapping, as it happens in every person.

With this conceptual broadening of the widespread biopsychosocial perspective, we add the recognition of the significant existential–spiritual dimension. It characterizes us as humans and includes all the other dimensions, in a kind of nesting. There is no way to experience meaning, freedom, responsibility, self-distancing, and self-transcendence without body, neurons, emotions, cognitions, mental dynamics, and intersubjectivity. For this reason, leading figures of existential psychology, such as the aforementioned Frankl (1946/2013) and Jaspers (1913/2012), May (1961/1991), Maslow (1962/2012), Yalom (1980/2015), and Schneider (2008/2015), have taken it upon themselves to state that it is not about pitting existential psychology against established psychologies (psychodynamic, cognitive–behavioral, or systemic) but about an existential psychology to complete a more comprehensive psychology. In fact, every psychological perspective has been able to illuminate some aspect of human subjectivity: the biochemical and neuronal correlation, the instinctual and psychosexual, environmental learning, cognitive processing, interactional bonding, the ability for self-realization and self-transcendence, etc. The problem lies in thinking that only one of those dimensions explains the whole. And the richness lies in integrating them into a vision as comprehensive as possible.

Pauline's relief comes through multiple intertwined paths. The illness, with its physiological consequences in the biological dimension, improves gradually, over a period of about a week in bed. Fears and anxieties are faced and diminished during therapy with the emotional support of the human encounter and through resources like humor. For example, in response to her frustration at not having friends or family to go to if she is hospitalized, the therapist reminds her that no person with COVID-19 can receive visitors during hospitalization, so it wouldn't matter if she had a ton of friends. At this comment, Pauline smiles for the first time. It can be said that at the core of this great fear of a lack of emotional ties lies an insecure attachment, manifested in the dependence on her ex-boyfriend, in the sadness that grows when she talks to her mother about her problems, in her demanding way of relating to friends and in her negative thoughts regarding the supposed negative assessment of her by colleagues at work. This bonding pattern has its origin in primary family conflicts: the early separation from her father and a depressive mother who was unable to hold her emotionally. Here we see the aspect of the emotional bond in the psychological and social dimensions. After achieving some degree of regulation of the emotional surges at the beginning of the crisis—from the secure base and validation built in the bond with the therapist—the existential questions and assessment begin.

After getting better, Pauline feels proud of herself for how she has been able to cope with illness and distress, realizing her attitudinal values. She also realizes that she has missed her students and her work:

She values the bond she has with them and the exchange that takes place within the context of teaching. She renews her commitment to teaching and to undertaking new projects related to composing and singing without depending on anyone to carry them out, as was the case in the past. She also decides to resume contact with friends she valued and had stopped seeing due to misunderstandings and her own excessive demand for attention (related to her insecure attachment). When, in the middle of 2020, worldwide protests erupted (that started in the United States) against racial discrimination and in defense of civil rights, Pauline decides to take part; feeling represented by this cause, she commits herself to it. By answering the questions that life asks her, which emerge especially in limit situations, Pauline commits herself to her process of becoming. To paraphrase Sartre, she decides what to do today, and in the future, with what others have made of her—for example, during her childhood. In other words, she decides to be the protagonist of her existence.

Our constant state of becoming is another fundamental aspect of the human being unveiled by existentialist philosophy (with roots that go back to Heraclitus's river). The bio-psychosocial-spiritual being that we are is updated and built at every moment and with every choice. Here resonates the well-known statement uttered by Sartre (1946/2016): "existence precedes essence"; that is, the individual "first of all exists, encounters himself, surges up in the world—and defines himself afterwards (...) is responsible for everything he does." This avant-garde existential gaze, based on the Heideggerian conception of being-there and being-in-the-world, breaks with millennia of essentialism and unveils vital subjectivity. Human freedom thus acquires its full meaning as a tool with which every person carves out their own existence. In this choice one makes for oneself, one chooses a humanity: "When we say that man is responsible for himself, we do not mean that he is responsible for his own individuality, but that he is responsible for all men" (Sartre, 1946/2016, p. 33).

Taken to the therapeutic level, James Bugental (1980/2008) explains that distinct levels of distress can be worked on. When patient and therapist dare to reach the very edge of the existential abyss, it is possible to go beyond repairing or adapting the way of being to transform it into a full exercise of one's own freedom. However, it is a road fraught with obstacles and crises.

Rollo May (1967/1987) takes the dynamics of subjectivity to its social and collective repercussions: "There is a dialectical relationship between social values and individual freedom, and we cannot have one without the other. Values are given and transmitted in the tradition of society and are constantly subject to affirmation, development, and re-forming by individuals in the society exercising some margin of freedom to affirm or defy" (p. 173). Times of crisis call for the courage to create new values that affirm more authentic ways of existence (in relation to the moment we are living).

What is at stake is the human responsibility to be free. And this freedom has different dimensions, connecting the collective to the individual and the existential to the other dimensions mentioned above. And we are not referring to unlimited freedom but to freedom in context, to being-there, to being-in-the-world. From a psychological point of view, Kirk Schneider (2008/2015) develops it clearly in his current existential–integrative proposal:

> Human experience (or *consciousness*) can be understood in terms of six (intertwined and overlapping) levels of freedom: the physiological, the environmental, the cognitive, the psychosexual, the interpersonal, and the experiential (*being*). These levels (or *spheres*) of consciousness reflect increasing degrees of freedom within an ever-deepening domain. The outermost (physiological) level, for example, is a simpler and more restrictive manifestation of the environmental level, the environmental level is a simpler and more restrictive manifestation of the cognitive level, and so on. (p. 35)

Can We Be Free in a Context That Limits Us?

The meaning of freedom should be explored in greater detail. The various levels of freedom described by Schneider (2008/2015) are located on the paradoxical continuum that has haunted humanity for as long as it can remember: free will and destiny, freedom, and limit. Diverse cultures and philosophies have often taken one side or the other. However, existentialism has walked the conflictive and fertile path of interbreeding since Kierkegaard (1849/2007): "Man is the synthesis of the infinite and the finite, the temporal and the eternal, of freedom and necessity" (p. 21). Heidegger (1927/2018) understood that only by recognizing his mortal destiny can the individual open himself to the vitality of the care of his being, to his authentic existence; that is, to the conscious being-there, and, therefore, to life itself. One of the questions we ask in this book is whether the global crisis unleashed by the pandemic could be a way for each individual and humanity itself to become aware of its mortality, and thus open itself to the question of its authentic existence. In other words, for the first time the entire world is taking part in some kind of sociological experiment in which we have all had to stop what we were doing and stay in our homes because of the threat of illness and death. This inevitable halt invites— we could even say pushes—us to reflect on our way of existing up to now. In the case of Pauline, who suffered the crisis both on a global scale and directly as an individual, this reflection emerged with full force. Are we exercising our freedom of being? Do we know that nothing is fixed, that we are in a state of becoming, and that, with more or less awareness, we create ourselves at every moment? As we become aware, will we continue on the same path or change course?

The Buddhist tradition, from which the perspective of full presence derives, recognizes the development of freedom in accepting the inevitable pain of existence, as well as in avoiding attachment to what is beautiful and pleasant about it. The Buddha said that pain is inherent to existence. From this perspective, the goal is "to learn to accept things with a kinder mind, changing what we can and receiving with an open heart what we cannot" (Reynoso, 2017, p. 53). Mindfulness is a practice that involves paying attention to the present moment as it happens without judging it or wanting to change it, even if it is uncomfortable. In this way, we are able to transcend our clinging to individual volitions.

Those who accept the ephemeral and finite nature of human existence will be able to develop further in it. Understanding that human suffering comes from denying the existential paradox, from clinging to the pleasant and rejecting the unpleasant, expands the capacity for compassion toward others and toward oneself. It involves internalizing our shared humanity, the human difficulty of accepting one's own condition, but also the human potential to transcend it. In other words, in its own way the perspective of full presence also finds the emergence of what is most human: In this case we could define it as freedom and compassion based on the acceptance of the present moment. This involves the acceptance of unavoidable pain and, thus, requires unlearning our clinging to individual volitions that reject it (and are the basis of all added mental suffering). Also from this perspective, the crisis of the pandemic shows us how ephemeral and uncertain life is, as well as the inevitable pain that existence can bring. Every person and community has lost something in this crisis. What will result from the fact that we have all lost the illusion of certainty?

The existential and Buddhist perspectives, which understand and consciously put into action the human paradox, developed psychological applications that have points in common as well as differences that may complement each other. One of the greatest insights of existential psychology has been that of Viktor Frankl's concept of meaning in inevitable suffering. When in life one is faced with an adverse and painful situation that cannot be changed, one can only change oneself, Frankl explains. Then, in the face of adversity, the individual will be able to choose their attitude in the exercise of their freedom and vital responsibility. In this way, it is possible to find a realization of meaning even in the worst situation. *Man's Search for Meaning* represents Frankl's own embodiment of this proposition: He recounts his own search for meaning as a prisoner in the Nazi concentration camps.

Regardless of how each person is experiencing or has experienced it, the pandemic has entailed a crisis in their own horizon and direction of meaning. Let us consider the plans and dreams that have been dashed: work, family, education, and social plans. But some changes in the context of the current difficulties may have been positive for some, such as spending less time traveling to work and more time with family. It inevitably calls for a rethinking of one's own meaning, for the present and the future as well.

Referring to Kierkegaard, Rollo May (1961/1991) defines (existential) anxiety as that which the person must face in order to develop their freedom and transform themselves in their growth process. Pathological anxiety appears when this vital challenge has not been faced. Kirk Schneider (2008/2015), a disciple of May, has further developed this paradoxical thinking, placing health and illness within an expansive–constrictive continuum of freedom and limit. Polar opposites lead to the pathological, while equilibrium and its paradoxical integration lead to full existence and freedom. This is freedom understood as the ability to choose within the boundaries of the specific context of life. Here we return to the theoretical approach to the historical pandemic situation: How has each person exercised their freedom in the limiting context posed by the personal–collective crisis?

In Pauline's case, we can speak, first of all, of freedom in the context of the viral disease itself. The freedom she had within the physical and social limitations during that time was to choose the attitude with which to face the situation. Because of the way she dealt with the situation, she felt proud of herself afterward. She also exercised her freedom to continue teaching and to produce musical projects within the limiting context of the pandemic. In other words, she accepted and adapted to the limits of what was present. Likewise, her reconnection with friends occurred within a series of virtual and then face-to-face encounters: She reconnected with friends she valued through social media like Facebook and then, as social isolation allowed, through in-person walks in the park. In order for this to happen, it was also important for her to become aware of her own difficulties with relationship anxiety (a limitation she had to recognize), which became less rigid with the emotional and cognitive regulation achieved during treatment—through the emotional scaffolding provided by the therapeutic bond during the crisis.

Jon Kabat-Zinn (1990/2016), from the Buddhist perspective of full presence, proposes embracing the crisis and total catastrophe that one suffers in one's life. This brings a twofold result: relief from suffering and greater openness to the possibilities of existence by learning to live moment by moment without clinging to the pleasant or rejecting the unpleasant. Francisco Varela et al. (1991/2011) argue that this way of experiencing life from full presence develops an experiential expansion of freedom and compassion. With regard to the first, it means freeing oneself from the suffering involved in the attachment to certainty and one's own individual volition, as well as opening oneself to different possibilities contained in the moment; with regard to the second, it involves understanding the roots of human suffering, transcending one's own individual experience, and developing a more open awareness that allows one to value the other person and their experience.

These perspectives promote the integration of the paradoxes of our existence and development of freedom in context (and its deployment of subjective agency) through acceptance, meaning, creativity, and encounter (Segafredo & Durao, 2021). The current human situation seems to call for this development, a question we still don't have answers to. Accepting, giving meaning, creating (oneself), and creating bonds involve being open to the question rather than securing an answer, which in turn may reveal new questions.

Being-in-Relationships: Individual–Humanity–World

Just as from the beginning we are thrown into existence, from the beginning there is a relationship to soften the blow, stimulate us, and participate in our becoming. There are different planes and layers to our relational existence. This is seen in the emotional–relational constitution of the self, proposed by authors like Winnicott

(1986/2011a; 1965/2011b) and Bowlby (1969; 2012); the always porous body–world interaction of Varela's neurophenomenology (2000); the human unfolding in the dialogical encounter with the other as explained by Buber (1923/2013); the humanity that we choose to be in the process of our subjectivity, according to existentialists and psychologists who take up this tradition; and, in a later movement, the planetary consciousness proposed by Morin (2020) from the intrinsic planet–humanity–person relationship.

All of the above is present from the moment we are born. The emotional bond with the mother (or the caregiver who fulfills this role), holds us, physically and emotionally, and presents the world to us. But primarily, the bond introduces us to ourselves. Because it is in the maternal care and gaze that we achieve sufficient integration to form our self, it is the starting point of the vital state of becoming (even of the later self-transcendence of the mature self). The emotional bond sustains the spontaneous gesture of the newly arrived tiny being and allows it to unfold its humanity in the conformation of a true self, sufficiently integrated to explore the world and participate in it. When the mother–child bond has existed to a sufficient extent, and, through it, the basic subjective integration, then the person will be able to feel real, to feel that they are (Winnicott, 1986/2011a; 1965/2011b). The child will have a secure base from which to venture out into the world. They will not be afraid to explore but will be enthusiastic because they will know they will always have a safe haven should they need it. The adult they become will also have confidence in themselves and their relationship with others and the world. And they will know how to find their emotional refuge when they need it (Bowlby, 1969/2012; 1973/1998).

Thanks to this bond of sufficient primary support, the person will then be able to go through the process of individuation. This involves a progressive separation and autonomy from the aforementioned maternal and paternal care and other predetermined structures. Once independence is achieved, which involves facing existential loneliness and the construction of oneself from the exercise of one's own freedom and one's own meaning, the human being is called to reconnect with the world and others, but from their creativity through work, love, art, and solidarity (Fromm, 1947/2007a).

Creativity from the true self is the genuine form of meeting and connection with the world, the healthy way to deal with anguish and existential isolation. It is vastly different from an undifferentiated fusion, such as that of the infant or the adult with severe pathologies.

There is also the pathology of the adult who submits to predetermined structures of meaning, leaving their freedom in the hands of others for fear of being. However, this is what generates the most anguish and vital dissatisfaction and, ultimately, pathology. Facing instead the existential anguish to transform it into creative living allows us to integrate, reunite with the world, and self-realize (Fromm, 1947/2007a; May, 1967/1987; Maslow, 1962/2012).

Likewise, every time we choose a more mature, broad, and inclusive existence or a regression toward a more self-centered and immature existence, we are somehow choosing a humanity. In other words, social consequences are generated. Fromm (2007b) proposed this process of individuation, maturity, and creativity of the person as the core of a more humanist, free, equitable, and just society. The person who develops their own humanity can understand that in it they contain the whole of humanity. On the other hand, it is worth noting that individuation and creativity as a reconnection with the world are constant processes in a person's life, unfinished, non-linear, and spiral. The experience of existential isolation (Yalom, 1980/2015) is inseparable from those processes as obverse and reverse, freedom and limit, or possibility and necessity, as Kierkegaard (1849/2007) would say.

The authentic I–Thou relationship (Buber, 1923/2013) allows us to transcend isolation and, at the same time, to return to it strengthened, to be able to accept it. Irving Yalom (1980/2015) takes up this concept to describe the therapeutic relationship as a healing refuge for the problem of existential isolation and as a space of reunion with the self through the bond with the other. The I–Thou bond is a dialogue and an openness to the other as a being, which involves a loving surrender to the encounter; it is contrary to the exchange in which the other is objectified and turned into a means of personal benefit, definable as I–It in Buberian terms. This I–Thou bond is a mutual recognition and an openness to participate in the existence of the other and to open one's own existence to the other. Martin Buber (1923/2013), the philosopher who developed this concept, summarizes it this way: "I become through my relation to the Thou; as I become I, I say Thou. All real living is meeting" (p. 13). The "I" itself emerges from the initial I–Thou, from the encounter, says Buber, in philosophical consonance with psychological studies of primary relationships, such as those conducted by Winnicott and Bowlby. In other words, for us to be able to say I, there has to be an

I–Thou first. After the I, and to unfold its development, there will also be an I–Thou.

Diego's case shows the importance of emotional bonds in the validation of one's own experience, especially if it involves pain, which, adds the need for support. Diego, a 25-year-old editor, begins psychotherapy on the recommendation of his doctors. They found no explanation for the unbearable pain in his mouth that keeps him from continuing with his daily work, family, and social life. They tried to medicate him with powerful painkillers and antidepressants and hypothesized trigeminal nerve neuralgia. Diego, who just moved in with his girlfriend, spends the day constantly putting ice on his face to numb the area. Some episodes have led him to stop working and even scream in pain. The only person who manages to calm him down a bit is his mother. He sometimes ends up hospitalized with oxygen to but goes home with no other diagnosis other than an inflammation that he seems to exaggerate. Hence the recommendation for psychological consultation.

In his first session, Diego can't stop crying. He is angry, tired of not being believed and of there being no solution. He presents several elements that indicate a state of depression. After an extensive account of his medical history, the therapist understands that Diego displays preserved reality testing and that his suffering is mainly caused by the invalidation of his pain. For this reason, he has been experiencing a worsening of his mood that opens the door to depression. The therapist decides to do the opposite of what was proposed by the doctors and returns to the physical symptoms. Diego's pain had to be addressed, both concretely and in its symbolic validation. A multidisciplinary effort begins with a medical doctor and a dentist who finally detect a series of signs leading to the discovery and removal of a tumor that was breaking the maxillary bone.

Instead of worrying about the cancer diagnosis, Diego is relieved. This is not only because after a year of discomfort and confusion there is finally a specific reason for his pain, but mainly because the therapist and other professionals have validated this experience of suffering. Diego needed another person to say *I believe you*, so that he himself could be sure that this experience was real. He also needed another person to say *I will help you*. Once the experience became an entity in the bond, he stopped feeling the emotional suffering of the invalidation, and only the physical pain remained, which was resolved with surgery and, later, chemotherapy.

Critical moments are those in which the person most needs the protection and reassurance of the bond (Bowlby, 1973/1998; Conangla, 2002). As a result of the validation and support provided by the therapist, Diego's mood not only improves but he also begins to have an awareness and a register of his emotions that he had never had before. After obtaining positive results from the chemotherapy, the pandemic appears, and Diego is once again worried about his health and the economic situation he and his girlfriend find themselves in. This time, he experiences his anguish without needing to turn to his mother. It is a great achievement for him, a sign of maturity.

Another aspect of our relational existence involves the dynamic interaction and interdependence between subjectivity and the world where one and the other intersect and co-construct each other. It occurs through the body that we are; cognition is embodied action, as Francisco Varela et al. (1991/2011) explain in their neurophenomenological proposal. Knowledge and mind emerge from bodily experience of the world, and the world also emerges from that same experience. By integrating Merleau-Ponty's phenomenology, Buddhist psychology, and cognitive sciences, Varela et al. (1991/2011) understand that "the world and the one who perceives it define themselves reciprocally" (p. 202). That is, environment and subject are shaped as the "mind and world emerge together in action" (p. 207). The human capacity to practice full presence—for example, through meditation—allows us to consciously open ourselves to that experience of indeterminacy and flow of mind and world, which we tend to ignore in our daily routine. This experiential and cognitive faculty, which lets us understand and transcend the ego perspective and thus deepen compassion toward otherness, includes the other aforementioned perspectives regarding our relational existence. It opens to emotional and existential intersubjectivity, to existentialist humanism, and to the emergence of a planetary consciousness.

Planetary consciousness involves understanding and experiencing the I–Thou in human nature, our earthly relational existence. This means being aware that "humanity is a planetary and biospheric entity" and, therefore, that "life emerges from the history of the Earth and man emerges from the history of terrestrial life" (p. 68), in the words of French philosopher Edgar Morin (1993; 2007/2010). This involves deepening our humanism even more, to learn to be-there on the planet. And so, we must assume our human and planetary community of destiny to which we are particularly called in this globalized era, where all the main problems have become increasingly transnationalized.

The coronavirus pandemic today occupies first place in an extensive list that has been written for decades: immigration, financial crises, environmental catastrophes, and transnational terrorism, among others. Here our relational existence occurs from individual to community to humanity and planet earth. The difference is that for the first time in history this latest crisis was experienced at the same time and with similar consequences in every corner of the world. Neither a country's GDP, nor its geopolitical hierarchy, nor the social class of an individual and their family have protected anyone (although in a second stage, countries with greater resources have been able to vaccinate and lower the number of infections and deaths in less time). Each person has felt the pandemic, the lockdown, and the emotional and economic toll in their body and in their entire subjectivity. The course of every person's life has been altered, as well as the community's, the whole of humanity, and even nature, which paradoxically has felt a respite. After the strict and initial isolation stage, nature decided to take to the streets.

Each person is a cosmos of emotions, longings, sensations, thoughts; humanity is all the people that constitute it, consciously and unconsciously; the planet is all the creatures that make it up; the cosmos, all the galaxies it contains. The cosmos represented by an individual is indivisible from the world: they occur together and at the same time. Heidegger's terminology of being-in-the-world involves a being that is inseparable from the world, which is (a state of becoming) at that moment linked to the world that surrounds it (physically and symbolically). "Human reality must be found at the precise moment of encounter between the being and the world. There is no humanity prior to such an encounter: human existence is a relationship" (Martínez Robles, 2012, p. 249). Could the current crisis, by highlighting this reality, be an alarm to awaken our relational existence?

What is already driving the pandemic is the inevitability of our relational existence. For example, the xenophobic expressions that initially arose toward the Chinese community, identifying them in a certain imaginary social construct as "carriers of the virus," have dissipated since all communities have been infected. Therein lies the unavoidable nature of emotional bonding and interdependence. However, this contextual determination is different from becoming aware of that relational existence and acting accordingly. In fact, the racism already in place has continued, such as that historically suffered by the African-American community. The issue returned full force to public debate in mid-2020, following the murder by a police officer of

George Floyd, an unarmed African-American man, and the ensuing mass protests in the United States and other countries around the world in favor of civil rights and against racial discrimination. It is interesting to think about how racism occurs even in the face of an emergency context focused on other issues that reflect our relational existence, and how the defense of human dignity occurs even in the face of the significant risk of contagion involved in marching in the streets in the midst of a pandemic.

We can embrace or reject, and even deny the bond with the other. What is certain is that we are related. Solitude itself, as a richness and sign of maturity, is defined by a previous internalized emotional bond that has allowed us to develop enough to have the capacity of being alone (Winnicott, 1965/2011b).

Our Existential Resources:
Acceptance, Meaning, Creativity, and Encounter

The existential–spiritual faculties involve potentialities of human development and resilience contained in each individual, even more so in the face of life's crises no are youmoment without judging it or seeking to modify it. This way of relating to the world is part of the modality of being, which is mentioned by both existentialists and experts on full presence. The two main modalities of human subjectivity would be that of doing and that of being. The first involves the planning and activation of a sequence of actions to achieve an objective and obtain specific results. There is nothing wrong with the modality of doing in itself, and it can be positive in some cases. However, it is not positive when it generates mental rumination or

> a recurring sense of unsatisfactoriness, reflecting the fact that the mind is focused on processing mismatches between how we need things to be and how they actually are. (...) The only interest in it is to monitor success or failure at meeting goals. The broader sense of the present, in what might be called its 'full multidimensional splendor', is missed. (Segal et al., 2013/2015, p. 126)

On the other hand, the modality of being involves "accepting and allowing things to be the way they are without trying to change them." There are no objectives or criteria as to how these should be. "It allows us to process in all its depth, breadth, and richness the experience of the present moment" (Segal et al., 2013/2015, p. 128). In the mode of being, there is no attachment to pleasant feelings and thoughts and no rejection of unpleasant ones. It allows us to have a decentralized perspective. And so, "there is a greater capacity to tolerate uncomfortable emotional states," and thoughts of how things should be, can be experienced as "mere mental events" (Segal et al., 2015, p. 129).

Mindfulness involves letting go of the need for total control, as well as the illusion of the permanence of things and the ability to "embrace total catastrophe" (Kabat-Zinn, 1990/2016). It enhances the acceptance of reality and, especially, of adversity. How much emotional and mental energy have billions of people spent complaining, denying, and fighting the inevitable global pandemic crisis? Regardless of the way in which we train and apply mindfulness, which is beyond the scope of this essay and which is dealt with in countless works such as those mentioned above, the capacity to be present and to accept the events of our existence lies in every person. In fact, from another perspective, the grieving process, which involves facing the emergence of a life-altering loss, is navigated (albeit relatively) once the person reaches the stage of acceptance (Kübler-Ross & Kessler, 2005/2018). The pandemic has brought concrete grief to people through the death of loved ones, but also symbolic grief from an important loss like a project, a job, an economic situation, a way of social life. The human ability for active acceptance is an existential faculty. We are not referring to conformity or resignation but to conscious and active acceptance. This in turn allows us to activate other faculties such as that of finding a new meaning.

Viktor Frankl, the therapist who most studied and applied the search for meaning as a form of healing and subjective development, understood that all life situations generate questions to which we are invited to respond. And the question always contains a meaning to be found. From this point of view, every human being's deepest driving force is the search for meaning, which far exceeds the relative attraction generated by pleasure. We may settle for homeostasis, but what vitally inspires a person is finding a mission or a goal worth striving deeply for, even postponing or putting aside pleasure. To this, Frankl adds that in every circumstance there is a singular meaning to be realized by each person. "We can also find meaning in life when we are faced, as a helpless victim, with a hopeless situation, with a fate we cannot change. What matters then is to bear witness to the best and exclusive human potentiality: that of transforming a tragedy into a personal triumph. When we are no longer able to change a situation—think, for example, of an illness such as an incurable cancer—we are challenged to change ourselves" (Frankl, 1978/2014, p. 41).

It is here where Kierkegaard's approach to the human paradox is expressed in its depth and breadth. Freedom and its (self-) transcendent action take power when we seem to be more cornered. Our own existential realization is more difficult, although more valuable and profound, in the face of a limit situation of unavoidable pain. This is what Frankl is referring to when he speaks of meaning in inevitable suffering: It could mean the opportunity to grow and exist in the best version of oneself. This does not mean being grateful for the adverse context but understanding that even when it is inevitable and cannot be changed, one can commit oneself to life. Frankl also explains that suffering is relieved when the person finds meaning—that is, some value that can be realized from the situation. Frankl sees himself as an example, recalling how he achieved some relief from the physical and emotional pain of forced labor in the Nazi concentration camps; he thought that this would serve to embody his theories about the power of meaning, and that in the future he could bear witness to what happened and help others to find meaning even in desperate personal and social situations (Frankl, 1946/1986).

In addition to accepting and signifying the adverse situation, there is also the possibility of creating from it, of transforming the anguish into something else, like an alchemy. In fact, the crises themselves are fertile ground for the creation of something new (Fernández Mouján, 1999). When there is a crisis, the structures and mental maps that have sustained our social roles, our way of being and our horizon of possibilities crumble. Only bare existence remains: oneself and what one values authentically (e.g., specific emotional ties). There are countless ways to rebuild what has crumbled. This is precisely the moment to embrace and create oneself from the most authentic position: being-there, as Heidegger would say.

In fact, creativity is a human faculty present from an incredibly early age, which helps to deal with life's difficulties and obstacles; but it is primarily an expression of the being-in-the-world that we are. It is the emergence of our subjectivity that creates the world while being created by it. It is the emergence of this intersection, a synthesis between subjectivity and the world. In principle, it occurs through children's play. Over time the game becomes more complex and becomes a sport, art, science, philosophy, religion. Winnicott (1986/2011a) explained some fundamental issues in this regard: that creativity is "the doing that arises from being" and that only a person's true self can be creative—that is, the one that arises and is built from the spontaneous gesture of the baby with the aforementioned good enough maternal care and scaffolding. This is how Winnicott sums it up (1965/2011b, p. 193): "The spontaneous gesture is the True Self in action. Only the True Self can be creative and only the True Self can feel real. Whereas a True Self feels real, the existence of a False Self results in a feeling unreal or a sense of futility." It is interesting to think of Winnicott's True Self as a psychological version of the authentic existence proposed by the existentialists, or rather that it is the expression of authentic existence from the dynamics of the psychological dimension.

In short, creative action involves modifying and assimilating the world from one's own authentic subjectivity. A child who plays is reflecting a healthy interaction between subjectivity and world, which involves a sufficiently integrated True Self.

> We find that integration into a unit does not mean that the individual has achieved peace. What the individual has achieved is a self which can contain the conflicts of all kinds that belong to the instincts and to the subtle needs of the spirit, and also the environmental conflicts which belong to the milieu. (Winnicott, 1986/2011a, pp. 256–257)

This integration of subjectivity is both cause and consequence of creative action. Every time a person experiences a crisis, they need to know that intermediate area of intersection between subjectivity and the world, where our being in movement emerges:

> It is assumed here that the task of reality-acceptance is never completed, that no human being is free from the strain of relating inner and outer reality, and that relief from this strain is provided by an intermediate area of experience which is not challenged (arts, religion, etc.). This intermediate area is in direct continuity with the play area of the small child who is "lost in play." (Winnicott, 1971/2015, p. 31)

A concrete example: Think of someone experiencing a sudden loss and how it can be transformative for them to express their anguish and their sadness by writing poems or dancing to a special song in which they pour out what they feel and what they miss. There occurs a sublimation, which is in itself healing. What the person feels is transformed into a poem or movements; the loss does not remain static but takes on vitality. Artistic expression is often a prime example; however, creativity encompasses any contribution a person makes to the world. This may be through solidarity, through work, through love. This transitional space embodies not only the elaboration of reality, the expression of the self and the intersection of inner world and outer world, but represents the meeting of individuality and world, the action of relational existence.

Erich Fromm (2007b) states that activating one's own creative capacity allows the individual to build a new connection with the world that synthesizes their relationship with others and their autonomous individual maturity, as well as the development of our humanity. Rollo May (1975/1994) considers that human creativity in all its expressions contains courage, because it gives life to what's new and unknown and has the power to energize collective values. In fact, the conflicting dynamic between social values and individual freedom allows the creation of renewed ways of being (May, 1967/1987). Once again, individual, community, and humanity are intertwined in a fractal structure in which the part contains the whole and vice versa. Creativity sets in motion the potentiality of becoming as human beings and as humanity. Culturally recognized artistic expression (which may represent the vanguard of changes in eras and values) is the literal manifestation of this dynamic; however, it constantly works at deeper and more deeply rooted levels in each individual's creative life: an entrepreneur, a carpenter, a social activist, a mother, a friend. Planning and carrying out an undertaking or a charitable action are the realization of a project, which in our society we understand as creative. However, authentic love, with its various forms of warmth and devotion to the other, is also profoundly creative. Let's consider a mother's creativity not only in the obvious playfulness that is explicit in a game, but in her presentation of food, of sharing and teaching language, of ways of showing the world. And let's consider, fundamentally, everything that is created from maternal affection.

Creativity participates in our process of accepting reality but also of signifying it, of giving it a shape and a meaning, especially of renewing our way of being-in-the-world. It is our relational existence with ourselves, the other, the world (in a symbolic sense what surrounds each one of us, and also literally planet Earth). Creativity involves action in terms of our becoming in our being-in-the-world. As May (1975/1994) explains, this occurs throughout a solid psychotherapeutic process at the individual level, but it also occurs with the changes that come with our current times at the collective level. We are currently facing a crisis, unleashed by the pandemic, which invites us to creatively confront our individual, collective, and planetary existence. The interesting thing is that the crisis is occurring at various levels simultaneously throughout the planet.

The capacity for encounter has already been sufficiently explained in the previous section on relational existence. It has to do fundamentally with a committed presence in our relationships, incarnated and activated from this awareness. In this encounter, there is acceptance, meaning, and creativity: acceptance of oneself, of the other, and of the encounter; meaning in terms of self-transcendence of oneself by turning toward the other and toward some common meaning; creativity in terms of creating the encounter, the bond, and a predisposition to participate and shape oneself. There is in the encounter a recognition of one's own relational existence with the other and the world. It is a loving action and awareness that recognizes and creates a virtuous feedback loop.

In this sense, psychology can make an important contribution, both in its psychotherapeutic practice and in the paradigm it contains. The essence and basis of psychotherapeutic work is to seek and build encounter: a self that is recognized and explored from the I–Thou therapeutic dyad.

Chapter 2

Humanity in a Limit Situation

It is undeniable that the pandemic has opened the door to a major crisis, which at the same time is a journey. As is always the case after a meaningful journey, we come back hugely different people, for better or for worse. Each one of us—those of us who write, those who read, all our relatives, the community in which we live, the country, the continent, the entire world—entered into crisis with the pandemic. It is an existential crisis akin to what Karl Jaspers called a limit situation: the collapse of the very structure of meaning that sustains daily certainties, reveals our naked existence in its anguished uncertainty, and, at the same time, has potential for creation and growth.

Limit situations always occur at some point in an individual's life, moments of high psychopathological risk studied in psychology and psychiatry as triggers or contexts of vulnerability to subjective and pathological distress. Throughout recent history, crises of this type have also occurred in communities and countries but very few times in a massive and simultaneous way all over the planet. The interesting thing is that this limit situation comes on top of a crisis of humanity that had already been detected decades ago, generated by an unsustainable economic and production system with disastrous consequences for the environment and for a vast majority of the population in ignorance, rejection, and denial of our relational existence. The pandemic and its lockdowns have forced a sudden halt to this (self-) destructive machinery.

Just as the pandemic highlighted the need to rethink this global structure, it also called into question the way in which each of us manages our daily lives. This is evident in the clinical psychology and mental health issues we face today. This does not mean, however, that as soon as there is a possibility of denying the underlying crisis (e.g., after mass vaccination), many won't try to erase it and return to everyday automatism.

The expansion of technology also plays an especially important role. The isolation caused by the pandemic has accelerated a process of virtualization of life in relation to health, work, family, and social relationships, which will have consequences that are still difficult to comprehend. In this regard, technology has offered a great possibility, for example, to maintain emotional or work ties, to continue communicating and engaging in relative activity even during isolation, in the two basic dimensions of subjective existence already pointed out by Freud: work and love (Erikson, 1950/1987). However, the fast-paced presence of technology in our daily lives—which will not retreat when the pandemic is over—apart from being a medium that channels human encounters, also brings with it several problems and risks to be analyzed. Technology as an end in itself carries the risk of pathology and dehumanization (the greatest of pathologies); along the same lines is its use as a powerful tool for manipulation. Technological excess and its conception as an end in itself somehow reproduces the self-destructive and dehumanizing impulse of the aforementioned machinery that has slowed down with the crisis.

Attempts to continue this outdated structure, regardless of the costs, are tantamount to a quest to overlap existential anguish with increasingly virtual entertainment products that reproduce a life that is not the real one. And, ultimately, the attempt by those who hold a paradigm of technology as an end in itself to replace the human with the machine, until absolute certainty and immortality are achieved. These risks predate the pandemic but are accentuated and evidenced by it.

At the root of the problem lie a void of meaning and a repressed and denied existential anguish. There is also a narcissistic, individualistic fragmentation, where otherness is unknown, and individual and world, mind and body, process and result are split in the illusory certainty of separation and compartmentalization of life. In short, it shows the ignorance and denial of our becoming and relational human condition.

The limit situation generates the opportunity to revisit our way of being-in-the-world. Aware that all the processes we are mentioning are occurring as we write, with a fate that is yet unknown, we nevertheless position ourselves in a commitment to recreate our way of being as individuals, as a community, as humanity. We recall the appeal made by Rollo May (1967/1987) to psychologists decades ago to put aside the obsession for conclusive results and naiveté regarding the management of power in the face of the nuclear threats and dehumanizing crises of that time: "The critical experiences of life, such as love, war, and peace, cannot come into being until we commit ourselves to them" (p. 168). He also called for this commitment to confront the problem of the dialectic between individual freedom and social values, both in and out of the therapist's office. What is happening today is that this conflict is raging both in and out of the office. The individual and society sense the need to review and re-create the values that guide their ways of being. And crises are fertile ground for this.

Technological Expansion:
A Possibility and a Risk for Relationship

It is worth contextualizing the current individual and collective crisis of the human being in its technological framework through two quotes that reflect the contrast between its lights and shadows. On the one hand, science fiction writer Arthur Clark says, "Any sufficiently advanced technology is equivalent to magic." On the other hand, we have Albert Einstein's appeal that "the human spirit must prevail over technology" (Hirsch & Durao, 2020).

Immediately after the pandemic, the vast majority of human activities and relationships were sustained not only through technology but also through virtuality, a new dimension it made possible (perhaps the fifth, if we consider time as the fourth). It is thanks to virtuality that people were able to come together in the context of a lockdown and social distancing. Many emotional bonds were kept alive and updated through this channeling. The virtual space made the I–Thou encounter possible.

In fact, in our clinical practice, we have been able to confirm the importance of this channeling. For several months in 2020, online therapy was the only viable way to continue any psychotherapeutic treatment in most countries of the world. In its synchronous and video-call version, this modality is in general a virtual channeling of the real human encounter between patient and therapist in favor of the relief of suffering and the patient's subjective development (Hirsch & Durao, 2020). When we say real encounter between two individuals, we refer again to Buber's I–Thou (1923/2013), with its respective therapeutic particularities.

The significance of this technological possibility takes on even greater dimensions in cases of patients who have suffered severe COVID-19 disease. Many have not only had to isolate themselves from the community but also from their loved ones. In addition to the suffering caused by this complete isolation, there is the fear and uncertainty as to whether they will ever see them again. In cases such as these, psychotherapy by video call provides emotional support that not only contributes to physical and mental improvement in the bio-psychosocial-spiritual beings that we are but also allows the person to even transform the process of this crisis into a possibility of rethinking life toward a more authentic existence. As in the case of Pauline, while she suffers from coronavirus, the therapeutic space allows her both emotional attunement and regulation, as well as support and significance of what is happening to her. The human dialogue channeled through the virtual medium helps her to reflect on her life and, among other things, to understand how important the bonds of friendship are to her. Once she is cured of the disease, she reconnects with friends through social media to meet again in parks and face-to-face meetings. She also discovers a vocation for civil militancy and joins the protests for racial equality and civil rights that took place in mid-2020 in Great Britain (as a repercussion of similar protests in the United States), whose community organized online. In this context, Pauline generates new bonds, which are actualized between the face-to-face and the virtual. Pauline's journey from online therapy to the face-to-face and virtual framework of her new bonds reflects, in short, the possibility of connection and human encounter offered by technology.

Technology's magical aspect makes it possible to transcend distances, both physical and symbolic, and generate new spaces for exchange. There is also the possibility of building collective meeting networks. In this regard, we can give some examples of things that have been implemented through virtuality, particularly during the pandemic: meditation networks, free psychological assistance (at the worst moment of the health emergency), and collective charitable actions. We have also witnessed small and simple altruistic gestures, like that of an Argentinian hairdresser who hosted live tutorials via Instagram to help hundreds of people dye and fix their hair during the strict lockdown.

The risk of technology, on the other hand, arises from the problem posed by Einstein: that it should not surpass or exceed humanity. That is, technology and its standardization should not become an end in itself; nor should we allow our dehumanization by losing ourselves in it. It's up to us, not the technology. In fact, it is a problem that goes beyond the technology itself. It has to do with developing and practicing what is most human: our being free and in relation—the recognition of one's own subjectivity, of one's own authentic existence in relation to the other and the world. This human reality is evident in the foundation of the therapeutic encounter: the person's need for validation of their own experience in dialogue with the other. Likewise, during the pandemic, it took on enormous significance in the oxymoron that the lockdown turned out to be: being isolated because we are so linked that from China to Argentina we share even our bodily weaknesses. However, if we do not consciously incorporate our relational existence, we run the risk that in the pandemic the other only becomes a threatening body, and in digital communication a mirror of our own narcissism.

The dynamic that digital social media facilitate by default is, paradoxically, very unsocial and narcissistic. If an individual does not approach another with the purpose of encounter (whether it is explicit or not) and with genuine shared interests, one tends to be absorbed by hypercommunication and hyperconnection with "everyone," which is void of relationship with someone. The main link is I–It, which by repeating itself so much ends up emptying the I itself of humanity, as a drowning of Narcissus in a bond that becomes It–It and, therefore, ceases to exist as a relationship. The philosopher Byung-Chul Han (2016/2019) explains the problem this way:

> In the digital echo chamber, in which the subjective spirit encounters nothing but itself, the Other is eliminated. Because of the absence of the Other, the voice of today's world is less audible. Unlike the You, the It has no voice (...) Bonds and interconnections are established without a gaze or a voice. In this they differ from relationships and encounters, which require the voice and the gaze. Moreover, they are special experiences with a voice and a gaze. They are corporeal experiences. The digital medium is decorporealizing. (p. 92)

In this case, decorporealization involves the concreteness of non-existence, the non-existence of a bond, and, therefore, the non-existence of subjectivity(ies).

We mustn't forget the importance of the body in human existence, which is to say, the direct and face-to-face experience of oneself, the other, and the world. In their neurophenomenological proposal, Varela et al. (1991/2011) explain subjectivity and its knowledge in the contact between body and world, in line with Merleau-Ponty. They speak of an embodied mind (the mind is in the whole body and is the body) in interaction and interdependence with the world. When the newborn experiences its subjective construction and its connection with the world in the physical and emotional bond with the mother, it is in the limit between the bodies that the recognition of oneself and the other is outlined (Anzieu, 1998). The I–Thou encounter is, at first, skin to skin. It is possibly on the basis of this leading bonding role of corporeality that we can understand how physicality facilitates (not ensures) the encounter.

However, the risk of a lack of physicality in the encounter is also reflected in current face-to-face contexts. The repeated image of two friends "meeting" face to face in a café only to sit across from each other, each engrossed in their cell phones and social media, speaks for itself. On the other hand, mothers and fathers may be in the same room as their babies or young children while leaving them connected for hours on end to the cell phone or tablet with videos tailored to soothe them (e.g., "Baby Einstein"). Not only is there a lack of contact and exchange with others, but the habit of spending hours with flashy stimuli on the screen leads to a lack of connection with themselves in two fundamental aspects: their own negative emotions such as boredom, as well as the creativity that awakens the game that the child invents with what is at hand. The subjective vitality of creative play is replaced by a passive reception of colors, music, and prefabricated stories that generate a quasi-hypnotic state, which instead of developing consciousness numbs it.

What is at risk here is the development of the self and, therefore, of the capacity for empathy, as well. Childhood is a fundamental and critical moment for this subjective construction, which continues to unfold throughout life. Sherry Turkle (2011/2017), a psychologist specialized in technology, relates the decrease in empathy registered in the younger generations over the last few decades with the permanent and excessive connection to the virtual world and with the bots that inhabit it, replacing human encounters and spontaneous conversations (a topic developed in the fourth chapter of this book).

As for the narcissistic dynamic facilitated by social media, Juan's case exemplifies this. He is a young man in his twenties, who at the start of the pandemic spends his lockdown with his family in a summer house on the beach. He battles with high doses of anxiety on a daily basis and produces countless photos of himself for his nearly 3,000 Instagram followers in order to become an influencer: he smiles, eats, exercises, and reads for the camera. At the same time, he begins to interact and play with his little cousin, who cries at night because he misses his mother, who is in another city. This crying leads Juan to an insight: For the first time, he feels that "those 2D connections," as he calls them in reference to their flatness, "are not real" and that "this guy who wants to look like an advertising model is not me." He also becomes aware of how these unrealistic bonds feed his anxiety circuit: the more he posts, the more he waits and checks the number of likes, the more anxious and empty he feels; to fill the void he posts again, and so on.

Juan very clearly describes the tendency to objectify these virtual spaces. In the images uploaded daily, Juan only shows himself as he wants his followers to see him—perfectly muscular and radiant in the middle of a pandemic—which is a means to raise his self-esteem." In none of the posts does he mention what he really goes through, feels, and thinks. Posting this idealized image is what the influencers that Juan follows and aspires to emulate do. The paradox is that anxiety rises with the dynamic of fake Juan's posts and the obsessive search for likes, which are never enough. This exacerbates the lack of encounter with oneself and with others; the emptiness increases and self-esteem decreases. On the other hand, when Juan plays in the family's backyard with his young cousin, he finds a "real 3D bond," as he calls it. Also, the sincere crying of this child because he misses his mother brings back the sense of isolation and abandonment that Juan felt at another point in time and that in a certain way he still feels. He is currently working, through video calls (here once again the light and the dark, which are not polar opposites but synthesis) with his therapist on how to create "three-dimensional bonds" with those around him: his parents, siblings, friends, and, therefore, also with himself. As Winnicott states, (1986/2011a, p. 43): "Being and feeling real belong essentially to health, and it is only if we can take being for granted that we can get on to the more positive things."

Juan's experience does not preclude the possibility that I–Thou bonds may arise from social media, as is the case with Pauline and her meetings with friends. It can happen, but just because someone "follows you" or follows the image you show does not mean that they "encounter you" and open up to you and vice versa. There is no dialogue in that observation. Nor will having thousands of "friends" on Facebook make them real friends; in fact, having thousands may mean not being friends with anyone. Hundreds of matches on Tinder do not mean building emotional ties with a partner; however, a date that comes from Tinder may be the first step in that direction. And, in the midst of the lockdown, Tinder (and other dating apps) has been one of the few "places" where you could meet people for dating purposes.

That said, the very dynamics of Tinder, where one likes (not chooses) based on a photo and a brief description, as if perusing products in the supermarket and as if one were a product, facilitates an exchange where in principle the other is not a subject but a means to feed one's own narcissism and satisfy one's own erotic pleasure. This initial dynamic may change, if the human disposition is transformed during the encounter (virtual or face to face), and the other becomes a You instead of an object (regardless of whether or not a lasting emotional bond develops). In fact, there is no shortage of people whose relationship has a virtual beginning, or at least a hybrid virtual/face-to-face one. Surely, since the pandemic, these cases will multiply. We can say that this context evidenced the historical change already in process regarding how people contact each other to establish erotic–emotional bonds (a topic that we will analyze in the next chapter).

On the other hand, there is a silent aspect to the narcissism facilitated by certain virtual dynamics: an endless experiential monologue where anything that is different is annulled, fed by the functioning of internet algorithms. "In the community of likes one finds only oneself and those like oneself," says Byung-Chul Han (2016/2019, p. 119).

"Robotic mode" is the term that Kirk Schneider (2017/2019) uses for the mental format that is activated when we are adrift in digital seas, and that lulls our consciousness into a kind of stupor: "Elemental reactions, narrowed perceptions, and rigidified assumptions about the world." This state leads to the reproduction of the new consumerist society, where the owners of social media make money with our time, and through increasingly invasive marketing are dedicated to bombarding us with ads, posts, and connections that respond precisely to our interests. This has been acknowledged by one of the founders of Facebook (Bilinkis, 2019), as well as by several regretful former executives at Google, Twitter, Facebook, Instagram, etc., in the 2020 documentary "The Social Dilemma, produced and streamed by Netflix, a platform that also uses algorithms and is part of that system (the episodes in the series come one after another in the TV-binging model we have all swallowed). We, the users, and our time and attention, are the product that generates the profits. And we allow this hypnosis with ourselves and become addicted to consuming (ourselves).

This stupor also creates a breeding ground for subtle (and not so subtle) forms of demagogy and political control, as well as the suspension of human spirituality with its capacity for wonder and becoming. In the era of hyperinformation, where we have unrestricted access to information and knowledge, the spread of fake news increases and circulates with everyone's participation. We tend to disseminate, casually and unchecked, information related to our prejudices and previous ideological beliefs. That is to say, there is a tendency toward a flat worldview, without contrasts, critical thinking, or otherness, where what prevails is the reproduction of information in which we believe beforehand.

The robotic mode and digital hypercommunication eliminate the mystery of life, the becoming, the capacity of choice in that uncertain context that comes with existence; they also lack the possibility of empathizing. Here we find the risk of dehumanization that the use of technology as an end in itself may mean, and the importance of recognizing it in order to find a way to integrate it as a means of human development. The worldview of hyperconnectedness and unlimited robotics involve the internalization of dehumanization and thus a false individuality and belonging (a false self, which is also inauthentic existence) surrendered both to technology (which is itself empty) and to the determination of others (those who dominate those technologies). These dangers are pointed out by Schneider in the extreme case of current movements such as transhumanism, which place technological progress above and even as the end of what is human (paradoxically, Schneider debates these issues through virtual meetings, recognizing the need for conscious use). In fact, adherents of transhumanism seek to adapt the human to the technological machinery, toward the unlimited, total control of life, anxiety, death, in a very distorted idea of freedom as absolute freedom, which cancels itself out. They seek, in short and among other objectives, the total control of emotions through psychopharmacological technology, the genetic improvement of each birth and the elimination of mortality through technological extensions of the body (replacement of the biological with the technological) in a radical Cartesianism where the mind goes on after the death of the body (Schneider, 2017/2019).

However, the pandemic once again showed the limit and the inevitability of the biological and the uncertain, embodying the mortal and the vital in the same *chiaroscuro*. What's unforeseen and what's different in nature burst in with this crisis, like a natural claw that pulls us out of our daily routine, technological virtuosity, and hyperconnectedness. And yet, in a paradox within a paradox, just as this crisis slows down our way of life, it also accelerates it. This happens with the virtualization of life and relationships.

On the other hand, the I–Thou encounter has become a pressing need during the pandemic due to its difficulty in the absence of presence (which facilitates it, although it does not ensure it); and it seems to have been sought and channeled much more than before through virtual platforms. This occurs at the same time as the stupor, narcissism, and empty hyperconnectivity, and even increasing communication with bots, as Sherry Turkle pointed out in an interview (American Academy of Arts & Sciences, 2020). The quest to be present with the other during the pandemic, albeit through virtuality, has accentuated our practices, capabilities, and forms of encounter channeled by technology, which is also linked to our confidence that this can happen. This is demonstrated, for example, by several therapists and consultants who were wary of online therapy and inevitably switched with satisfactory results to this modality (Hirsch & Durao, 2020). Also, meditation instructors like Martín Reynoso, did this with groups of mindfulness practitioners and work with presence in the here and now (Durao, 2021). This collective search for encounter in the virtual space represents a quite different trend from the problematic narcissistic and inauthentic dynamics described above, in a struggle of opposing cultural and subjective forces of uncertain outcome. Likewise, this renewed willingness could nurture awareness of the value of genuine human encounter. Perhaps from now on we will stop taking for granted the possibility of encountering one another, and also our projects. Will social isolation allow us to appreciate the richness of the human encounter, which we had forgotten in the widespread pre-pandemic absent presence (the classic example of the two friends in a café, each on their own phone)? From now on, when we meet face to face, will we do so without being distracted? Could something similar happen to us with respect to the encounter with nature and the environmental urgencies of the times?

Regardless of the answers we may have to these questions, we know that the technological power of our time presents intertwined challenges, possibilities, and risks that call for a renewed humanism that consciously includes it.

Global and Singular Limit Situation

In an interview months before the pandemic (Segafredo, 2020), Alfried Längle, one of the current leading experts on existential analysis, said that the deep environmental crisis of recent years and the risk of human extinction contained therein could not be interpreted as a limit situation of humanity in a global sense. His explanation was that despite the existence of a crisis, it was too abstract, that mortality had yet to be felt in the body. It had to become tangible. The pandemic precisely brought that: the anguish of bodily death on an individual scale and the anguish of cultural death (as a way of life) on a collective scale. There was uncertainty regarding one's own health and the possibility of becoming ill, awareness of one's own mortality as individuals but also uncertainty regarding the continuity of the human way of life. There was also a forced and astonishing awareness that humanity's form of existence, as it had unfolded until then, would neither last forever nor remain unchanging.

Several articles have analyzed the pandemic and its consequences as a limit situation (Méndez, 2020). But what does this mean in each of our lives, in the experience of humanity, and in our relationship with the world, with one another, and with nature? These are different planes, intrinsically linked, interconnected, and nested, which co-construct each other (Morin, 1993; 2020). Erich Fromm's (2007b) statement that every person contains all of humanity, like the part of a hologram that holds the information of the whole, is enlightening:

> I carry within myself all of humanity; that, in spite of the fact that there are no two individuals who are the same, the paradox exists that we all share in the same substance, in the same quality; that nothing which exists in any human being does not exist in myself. I am the criminal, and I am the saint. I am the child, and I am the adult. I am the man who lived a hundred thousand years ago, and I am the man who, provided we don't destroy the human race, will live a hundred thousand years from now. (pp. 102–103)

We may dwell on the last part of Fromm's quote. First of all, it reminds us that several thinkers have been warning us about this danger for decades. Then, it leads us to question ourselves about what it means to become aware that we are in danger as a species (both in terms of an actual extinction like that of the dinosaurs, and also an extinction of that which makes us more human). Could the same thing happen on a collective scale that occurs when a person finds themselves (in reality or symbolically) facing their own mortality and is able to transform anguish into a reassessment of the authenticity of their existence and values (Yalom, 1980/2015)? It is worth returning for a moment to the Jaspersian origin of the subject, with its focus on individual experience.

Karl Jaspers explains that the limit situation opens an existential abyss in the sequence of ordinary situations, where the person falls from their axis of continuity, from their construction of reality, and this is revealed as it is: an assemblage with illusions of certainty and security that denies finitude and vital dynamics. It is a human experience of vertigo when faced with naked existence after the dissolution of everyday life. Limit situations mean facing death, struggle, guilt, and chance as inevitable in human existence. The experience of these situations involves suffering and awareness of one's own finitude, and especially a lack of foundation and support from experience and thought (Jaspers, 1919/1950). "Neurosis has been considered a failure in the face of limit situations; and the goal of therapy is the self-transformation of the human being who through limit situations comes to an understanding of themselves" (Jaspers, 1913/2012, p. 358). Here arises the paradoxical character of limit situations, related to the tragic potential darkness and the lightness of human existence so well defined by the statement of the master Kierkegaard (1849/2007): "The self is a synthesis of the infinite and the finite," where possibility and necessity meet in the concrete becoming of oneself. It is a paradox of our subjectivity, translated in its current psychological application as limit–freedom and expansion–constriction of the self (Schneider, 2008/2015).

It is at the limit of their existence that the human being is free and responsible for realizing this freedom in all its potentiality. "That which the human being really is and that which they can become has its origin in experience, in the acceptance and overcoming of limit situations" (Jaspers, 1919/1950, p. 353). In the limit situation of death, authentic life emerges: in randomness, meaning; in struggle, serenity; and in guilt, responsibility. This is also linked to the main contribution of the renowned Viennese psychiatrist and neurologist Viktor Frankl (1946/1986): the possibility of finding meaning in situations of unavoidable suffering, and of responding to adversity with a deepening of existential authenticity. The greater the difficulty, the greater the potential realization.

On the other hand, in limit situations the double human inclination is expressed: the knowledge and exercise of their creative and developmental responsibility, together with the tendency to nothingness and the security of previous structures (Jaspers, 1919/1950). Once again, risk and opportunity are present: the risk of stagnating in something that is no longer functional for the person, which may start as a vital problem and reach psychopathology; the potential for self-transformation and development of the person in their dynamic becoming. Jaspers explains that "the wrappings of the ways of life" need to be transformed so that a person's subjectivity in their relationship with the world can unfold. This transformation occurs thanks to limit situations that defy the known construct so they may launch themselves into their own uncertain creation. This understanding of the human being includes Heraclitus's ancient and ever-present statement regarding the inevitable flow of existence. On a less profound level, it also refers to the Piagetian formulation of the development and maturity of intelligence and its capacity for abstraction (Piaget & Inhelder, 1969/2015). However, Jaspers speaks of a subjective development that continues throughout life, that in the physiological and cognitive dimension could also be linked to neuroplasticity.

The fundamental limit situation of death manifests an inevitability of everything that exists, from the micro-constellation represented by an individual to the set of constellations that make up the Milky Way galaxy, which includes the planet Earth. Everything real is transitory. At the level of the individual, we may exemplify this with, among other things, the presence of loved ones, the bond with a partner, a productive work situation, and, first and last, life itself; everything is born and dies. It is a truism, often forgotten in the hustle and bustle of everyday life, although the crisis brought on by the pandemic has reminded us of this. Perhaps it might be useful not to constantly think about expiration, to avoid the anguish it evokes during the daily resolution of ordinary situations. However, it is extremely dangerous to live life as if there were no end; you run the risk of forgetting to focus on what you value most. The daily a-mortal construct comes along with low tolerance for frustration and the need for immediate reward, which is fed by contemporary technological constructs. Frustrations involve recognizing impermanence and limits, just as the process involves understanding that there is a beginning and a development to reach an end.

The denial of impermanence is often the cause and consequence of automatism and emptiness of meaning, a clinical and cultural problem that Frankl (1977/2003) pointed out throughout the second half of the 20th century and that many existentialist psychologists today consider to be current and even increasing. However, the limit situation of death pushes us to get out of this daily a-mortal construction and to understand life in its paradox. Yalom (1980/2015) verifies this in his extensive clinical experience with oncology patients: "A confrontation with one's personal death ('my death') is the nonpareil boundary situation and has the power to provide a massive shift in the way one lives in the world (...) Shifts one away from trivial preoccupations and provides life with depth and poignancy and an entirely different perspective" (p. 195).

A person's vital process finds in limit situations essential turning points for its dynamics in the unfolding and transformation of subjectivity. At the same time, limit situations contain suffering and great risks. They are forks in the road, which can mean enriching oneself with the discovery of new worlds but also risking getting lost in the forests of anguish and walking in circles without finding the way out. In short, the urgent experience of a limit situation involves the idea of one's own death, the collapse of fundamental structures, the rethinking of one's own values and important decisions.

The limit situation triggered by the pandemic may have brought awareness of finiteness. But it also brought the surprise of its sudden and random arrival (beyond conspiracy theories and whether someone had really actively participated in the creation of the virus and the pandemic). In addition, it brought a paradigm of almost warlike struggle regarding the confrontation of the virus and the awakening of questions regarding our guilt about the situation (e.g., in relation to the mentioned environmental problem and the images of its vitality in the face of our absence). This limit situation contains, therefore, the various limit situations mentioned by Jaspers; it is thus of critical and existential depth, as much in its dimension of danger as in that of opportunity. This entails much suffering, which has also manifested explicitly in illness and death; in hunger and destitution; in massive psycho-emotional sufferings of anxiety, stress, and complicated grief. It calls for a rethinking of the way of being-in-the-world as a person and humanity.

In individual terms, we may present Marta's particular case, which not only involves a rethinking of one's own existential authenticity based on the limit situation and inevitably adds the variables of bonds and technology. Marta has been a homemaker for years. She is unsure of herself and has had frequent panic attacks for years, accompanied by some depersonalization. The pandemic wiped out her husband's business and threw the family into crisis. The economic urgency thus led Marta to go back to her studies as a primary school teacher in an online training and to give virtual classes as a private tutor. With this, she revives a vocation she has always had. In the limit situation of the pandemic, Marta's family structure flounders, and this generates suffering. However, it also allows Marta to break out of the preestablished patterns and roles and awaken to existence and its dynamics, to use her ability to create herself in context, to take responsibility for her freedom (the role of homemaker she has occupied by inertia, not by choice). In other words, it allows her to become the person she is and to leave behind the depersonalization she felt in the trap of inauthentic existence into which she had fallen.

The fear of freedom is not an easy thing, as Fromm brilliantly explains in his classic work; however, once we face it, our own authenticity unfolds, and that realization dilutes much of the anguish. And so, in Marta's sessions she stops talking about panic attacks and depersonalization to give space to her teaching vocation and her online private lessons. Here, the limit situation as a context and technology as a tool enable Marta's new professional development. Especially because of the unalterable circumstance of lockdown, marketing on social media does not mean a sudden and abrupt presentation to the world as face-to-face promotion would have been. And this progressive journey, which Marta needed, could culminate in future in-person classes in schools. Marta's development process even improves her bond with her husband. In the past, she felt like she was less and at a disadvantage; however, since she is now supporting the family together with her husband (who got a different job than the one he had before the pandemic), the bond becomes complementary and stronger. Crises modify our particular and relational existence, and often highlight its unfolding.

A Call to Create and Relate with One Another

Just as Martha was living in anguish (as a latent crisis) for years, humanity has been in crisis (symbolically and concretely) for decades. But the crisis and its anguish have never become so real and corporeal on a global scale as during the pandemic; nor has relational existence been so manifestly evidenced in the past. So far, the environmental and social disasters of our unsustainable production system have not reached or endangered our bodies. Although there are occasionally environmental catastrophes that remind us that the Earth is in danger, for most of humanity these catastrophes occur in "faraway places." Although destitution affects huge populations, for those of us who do not suffer from hunger it remains far away. In fact, a denial of this reality and of the inevitable need for transformation is reflected in the widespread election of extremist conservative leaders who have promised a return to old, antiquated patterns. Some of these leaders have been the worst in handling the recent pandemic crisis.

However, what has happened with the pandemic and its lockdowns is that much of humanity has experienced the crisis and its associated drama simultaneously. Neither social class, national GDP level, nor the region's position in the geopolitical hierarchy has exempted anyone. On the one hand, the virus forced us into isolation, but it also brought humanity together in this shared experience. It endangered life itself and also the life of humanity as we knew it. On the flipside of the lockdowns, nature had a respite, which in a way meant that we had a respite from ourselves. Thus, the false dichotomy and human–nature separation was highlighted in this contradiction. The same happened with the false dichotomy of I–other. We don't mean undifferentiation, but re-union, of interdependence and inter-relational existence: "Existence begins from a relationship, and everything we are emerges from inter-relational networks (...) We are in relation to the physical and surrounding world; and in relation to others who are, at the same time, similar and different from us" (Martínez Robles, 2012, p. 197). Being-in-the-world, being-with-others, being-in-relationship: We are in relation to our ancestors and to those to come after us. What we choose to be, to become, the way we (re)create ourselves, the way we bond with one another and the world will be a choice for all those who are, for those who have been, and those who will be. To become aware of this and to act upon it already involves a great transformation. According to different thinkers, the abyss facing humanity has to do with dehumanization and ignorance at various levels of this relational existence (Morin, 2007/2010). There is still a clinging to an outdated Cartesian and modern individualist paradigm and to its fragments left in certain postmodern forms of hyperindividualism (Lipovetsky, 1983/2014).

The suffering and uncertainty brought on by the pandemic has been clear for the infected and their families, for the hardest hit countries, and for all those socioeconomically affected; but in some sense, more or less directly, it involves each one of us. The risk lies in being trapped in fear through individualistic, balkanizing spasms of an "every man for himself" type of nationalism. On a personal scale, a simple example of this may be the initial compulsive stocking of cleaning products and food items that left others without. This has been replicated, among many other things, on an international scale, in some cases with similar attempts regarding medicines and vaccines (later solidarity networks also appeared in this regard). However, as has been said since the beginning of the century in the field of international politics: Faced with this globalized world, the new realism involves a cosmopolitan relational outlook (not to homogenize but to bring together in plurality), planetary awareness, and cooperation in the resolution of transnational problems; otherwise, no one will be saved (Beck, 2005; Morin, 2007/2010; 2020). Today, there is no longer any way to deny the fact that we are all inevitably in the same boat (Zizek, 2020). Therein lies the opportunity.

This limit situation highlights both the existential crisis that the human species has been going through in the last few decades, as well as our inescapable relational existence and becoming. So, the opportunity could be, primarily, to deepen our compassion and bonding, to recognize our relational existence. What happens to the other is no longer far away. Shared humanity becomes present and invites us to humanize our fast-paced global reality. The isolation into which we have been forced is an oxymoron. The suffering that occurs in another house, another city, another country, or another continent affects us; whether we like it or not, it is also our suffering. It is a fact. We are connected on multiple levels, from something as basic as the air we share and the environment in whose encounter our being emerges.

From this recognition of our relational existence, we can consciously commit ourselves to our becoming and take advantage of the field of creation of the crisis (Fernández Mouján, 1999), which in this case has an enormous, global potential. We can review and rethink the authenticity of the life we lead and the humanity we are. It is an authenticity referred to the present moment we are living, as a person, humanity, world. The previously mentioned case of Pauline serves to exemplify this. Her subjective authenticity increases as a result of the transformation of the limit situation; the conscious appreciation of aspects of her life that were covered up or blocked, such as work fulfillment and friendships, emerges in her. Together with this same process of encounter with herself and with the other, she also makes a choice of possible humanity, which finally even becomes explicit through her militancy against racial discrimination. Pauline thus creates new possibilities of bonding with herself and the world from her renewed and chosen way of being.

Fromm and May put forward, each in their own way, remarkably interesting conceptualizations of creativity. May (1975/1994) speaks of the courage to create as an existential daring into the unknown, in the discovery of new ways and values through which a person and a society can be transformed. Fromm (2007b) posits creative living as a way of reconnecting with the world and others after achieving one's own individuation and autonomy. It is a conscious return to the bond (in principle it was always the relationship, as Buber or Bowlby would say, on various levels), but from a responsible freedom and with a contribution from the particular way of being-in-the-world. It may be interesting to think and act today with a courage to create, to consciously reconnect with the other and the world, from self-awareness. Maybe the time has come for this to happen on different planes of the person–community–humanity–world fractal.

This is not something that in itself will occur from the limit situation implied by the pandemic but is a creative possibility that comes up. Any clinical psychologist in the world knows very well that in contrast to cases like Pauline's, there are many others who, after the individual and collective limit situation generated by the pandemic, have sunk deeper into anguish or have taken refuge in denial as soon as circumstances allowed (after having been cured of COVID, for example, or with the lifting of restrictions and a personal economic upturn). Risks are also present on a societal scale. On the one hand, when faced with any sign of certainty such as that which mass vaccination seems to bring, a return to daily denial and automatism is tempting as a Pyrrhic victory; the illusion of returning to pre-pandemic "normality" is thus spread and revived. In the same vein, there is a risk of deepening individualism, narcissism, fragmentation, and emptiness in this. On the other hand, there is an expansion of biopolitical control and a subtle authoritarianism that could take advantage of individualism and emptiness, take the path of dehumanization, and reactivate the unsustainable economic machinery, which had a hiatus with the pandemic and reflects the way of life of the last few decades. As Byung-Chul Han (2020) states, "no virus is capable of causing the revolution (...) it is we, people endowed with reason, who have to rethink and radically restrict destructive capitalism, and also our unlimited and destructive mobility, to save ourselves, to save the climate and our beautiful planet" (p. 111).

In other contexts, analyses can be made on how to materialize in multiple political, social, economic, and cultural dimensions the recognition and strengthening of our relational existence and responsibility in the creation of our becoming: for example, how to foster planetary awareness based on the principle of "not only but also" (Morin, 2007/2010; Beck, 2005), politically democratize globalization in a contextual way, generate a sustainable production and living system. From psychology and the repercussion that each subjectivity has in the community (local, national, human, planetary), we can speak of the reappraisal of the true encounter. This occurs in emotional bonds but also in other social and potentially supportive bonds, such as those built with a study or work partner, a neighbor or a stranger, and the true encounter in contact with nature. That is, contact with otherness: the human other and the planetary other. Here the body has a significant role that we should not forget since, as mentioned by Francisco Varela et al. (1991/2011), the subjective experience of contact with the other and the world is corporeal; virtuality complements but does not replace it. To put it in simple, common-sense terms, we mean learning to listen and spreading the listening.

The clinical psychologist is, at best, a professional listener. Their challenge is to really listen to the person who consults, who, in time, learns to listen to themselves, and, in this way, learns also to listen to the other. By practicing listening, the psychologist should indirectly spread the practice and not monopolize it as a private professional practice, so that listening can become public. This could be a contribution of psychology to the necessary regeneration of community: "Listening has a political dimension. It is an action, an active participation in the existence of others, and also in their sufferings" (Han, 2016/2019, p. 121).

Existential–integrative psychologist Kirk Schneider (2017/2019), explicitly applies the experience of the human encounter practiced by psychotherapy to different sociopolitical projects of dialogue between people with diverse partisan orientation. He has promoted it in meetings between common citizens of opposite political paths, together with the group *Braver Angels*, to facilitate from the human presence with the other the points they have in common and the understanding of their perspective. It has also been disseminated in U.S. decision-making spheres, as in the case of the practice he calls Experiential Democracy, which he describes in this way:

> I seek to generate meetings between legislators, those who make major decisions about our lives, to make it easier for them to really listen to each other. Primarily, they would be sitting face to face, to avoid rhetoric and the influence of lobbying and dogmas. My hope is that people can see the humanity in each other, beyond the media images and stereotypes. The intention is to learn from each other, with a phenomenological perspective, to avoid the continuation of polarization cycles.

> From there, we need to look for common ground that may lead
> to new thoughts about each other or actions. (Segafredo, 2019,
> p. 50)

The interesting thing about the case is that during the pandemic, Schneider has held webinars on these projects, promoted through social media. The technological functionality is so inevitable, that it becomes necessary to use even to spread a critique of its excessive use and prominence.

On a more daily and silent level, fathers and mothers (or caregivers who fulfill this role) who affectionately support their children, perform this humanizing listening that is so necessary. Through this bond, parents teach their children to identify and regulate their emotions, to tolerate frustration and, by example, to include the other in their world until they achieve the miracle of empathy. This awareness of oneself and of the other is not transmitted by technological devices, which in their dysfunctional use feed states of semi-awareness and stupor far removed from the construction of a true self, from the presence and creativity that this entails. Fathers, mothers, and caregivers fulfill with these children a corporeal role and emotional bond of listening, fundamental not only at the family level, but also at the social and political level. Decades ago, Winnicott (1986/2011a) spoke of the importance of the role of the good-enough mother for the construction of a democratic society: "We know something of the reasons why this long and exacting task, the parents' job of seeing their children through, is a job worth doing; and, in fact, we believe that it provides the only real basis for society, and the only factory for the democratic tendency in a country's social system" (p. 144).

In this same line of social contribution, psychology (in the clinic and in other fields such as education, labor, etc.) can nurture in people the courage to imagine and realize the creation of new ways of being that recognize their becoming in the expansion of their authenticity and their link with otherness, which go hand in hand. Psychology can also nurture the search for and construction of meaning in each person and at each moment, as well as the stimulation of existential resources and the ability to meet (whether in person or virtually). The self is found when it goes out of itself and goes toward the other or the other thing, in the self-transcendence that occurs through love, solidarity, a cause, a project, a horizon.

Activating the modality of being, the capacity to listen, and the capacity to create (ourselves) will give meaning and response to the unknown adverse circumstances that have arisen since the pandemic. And, in the same movement, deepen our humanity.

Part 2

New Ways of Living and Forms of Mental Health

Chapter 3

Isolation and Virtualization of Life

The crisis brought on by the pandemic in its intersection with the particular and rapidly changing social and technological context has challenged and shaken the foundation of our way of life. Although change is still ongoing and there are many areas undergoing transformation, we will present three fundamental aspects of human life—education, work, and love—that have developed in numerous ways since the beginning of our history and whose change is evident today both in the therapeutic field and in the lives of the vast majority of people. Likewise, in light of the recent virtuality of these dimensions, we delve into what is happening to corporeal presence, since human experience is inevitably embodied. From this embodied awareness, we also approach our critical relationship with nature, which surrounds us and constitutes us, from which we differentiate ourselves and of which we are a part.

The Two Sides of Virtual Education

The pandemic and social distancing have deepened the digitalization and virtualization of schools, universities, and other educational institutions. As in other areas of life, there has been a rapid and forced expansion of technology. The process was already underway but at a different speed, both for better and for worse. On the one hand, the constant progressive pace allowed for a more measured, culturally integrated, and contextualized inclusion; on the other hand, that pace also justified a certain structural technological outdatedness of some educational institutions.

Faced with this panorama of sudden and dizzying global virtualization of education, the Futures of Education International Commission (2020) of UNESCO prepared a report that highlights the urgent issues that need to be resolved in order to uphold the human right to education. The goal is to find a way to reverse the digital gap, which includes 50% of the world's population with no computer at home and 40% with no Internet connection. The technologies used for education need to be freely available, open source, and not dependent on private companies. We need to develop digital tools and content based on the teacher–student (and, we may add, student–student) human bond. It is important to protect and not relinquish the school as a space and time of face-to-face interaction, even when it includes the virtual aspect. These are some of the report's many points, which include revaluing science, the accuracy of information in times of ever-growing fake news, as well as the addition of an ecological perspective.

First of all, we will focus our attention on the school, where we encounter the most pressing problems. Recent studies have shown how the suspension of face-to-face classes have had negative effects on the mental health of children and adolescents, especially with respect to attention problems and disorganization in daily routines. In addition, it has also increased anxiety, irritability, and dependence as a consequence of the overall social isolation (Marques de Miranda, et al., 2020). Likewise, neuropsychologist Carina Castro Fumero explained in an interview on the Instagram account Tanconectados (2020) that another fundamental problem in isolated elementary school children is the lack of physical movement, which has undermined their neuroplasticity. The reason is physical movement (whether through sports, recreational activities, etc.) fuels the production of BDNF (Brain Delivered Neurotrophic Factor) protein, which in turn facilitates neuroplasticity and thus learning.

Regarding virtual education in particular, undergraduate and graduate university studies involve a subjective stage in the individual, which in connection to virtuality may be more beneficial and less critical. Functionally speaking, and following the Piagetian stages (Piaget & Inhelder, 1969/2015), we may say that as the capacity for abstraction is acquired and increases, learning requires less of the body and matter as a base; not only do we stop depending exclusively on the body, but, in part, the corporeal experience we've already been through may be re-created in virtuality. It is worth adding that in one way or another, the body is always part of our relationship with the world because of our embodied mind (Varela et al., 1991/2011).

On the other hand, the infinite library made possible by today's online digital technology is one of humanity's greatest advances in the democratization of knowledge. Likewise, with virtualization, training is federalized. Someone living in a remote area may have access to the same educational and cultural resources as someone who lives in a big city. Technology expands tools and possibilities in both teaching and learning: accessible content in different formats, as well as collaborative production, synchronous and asynchronous exchange, etc. However, technology in and of itself does not contain a fundamental aspect of education, either at the social or individual level: the encounter and the human bond with the other and with oneself, the construction of community and of the person as such, based on certain individual and shared values.

Something that is also fundamental in psycho-pedagogical terms is that the social constructivist perspective recognizes the bond as the basis for learning, because it is through this relationship that the zone of proximal development is generated; it is the dyadic space where the learner can express and develop that which is still a potential but which, thanks to the bond, will become an increasingly autonomous reality. The same higher psychological functions that the individual acquires, such as language, are in the first place, a social bond between people (Vigotsky, 1934/2012). At the same time, in this encounter, the individual not only learns to know and to do a certain thing but learns to be and to experience their shared humanity (with the other), which is ultimately also a shared planetary awareness (with the other and the world). It is in this human bond that education embraces its four pillars: "learning to know, learning to do, learning to live together, and learning to be" (Futures of Education International Commission, 2020). Education thus develops its planetary humanist sense: the unfolding of being in becoming and in relation.

In virtuality, which has allowed the magic of maintaining virtual school contact during times of pandemic and isolation, this educational dimension of our relational subjectivity must be constantly worked on, without taking it for granted. Otherwise, it could end up enabling a more or less explicit management of education based on the interests of private technological companies that, like any business, respond to their profits.

Several education specialists have put forward different ideas so that virtual education may recreate the fundamental teacher–student encounter with its human values. Daniel Brailovsky (2020) is one of them:

- If we have to communicate through forums and chats, let's try to make our communication as similar as possible to a text, a letter, a personal story.
- If we are to promote tasks through computers and cell phones, let's make them critically reviewed, with the possibility of

exchange, of a back and forth that is as fluid and sensitive as possible.

- Let's propose writing games in the digital spaces we provide for writing. Let's make room for humor wherever it can be found.
- Let's promote exercises linked to note-taking during our live classes by Zoom, Meet, or any of these systems currently being used.
- And let's not forget that the material nature of the classroom can be recovered by calling upon its characteristic objects: the blackboard, the notebook, the book. We can stand in front of the camera, open a book, share a text fragment, discuss. Ask questions.

The feeling of fatigue that comes with making these efforts to include the encounter and its material nature as a presence has been experienced by teachers and students alike. It also occurs in other areas, such as psychotherapy.

Few doubt that from now on education will be hybrid, face to face and virtual. However, it is important to consider the development of the person's subjectivity in relation to the balance of this complementarity. The younger the age, the greater the need for a physical face-to-face bond. If we're talking about postgraduate or specialization courses, for example, for decades now the model has been a periodic but spaced-out face-to-face presence, and the virtual aspect occurs explicitly in a digital platform or in the classic and asynchronous reading of bibliography, which also has a virtual dimension in terms of representation of other material realities (as is the case in language and every symbol). A balanced postgraduate specialization therefore requires less face-to-face attendance and allows for more virtuality (some have shown good academic results even with an entirely online format).

Meanwhile, a balanced school education requires a high degree of presence and less virtuality (used only as a tool that reinforces what is done in presence). This is related to the interaction of variables that we may call holding and autonomy, which are not only related to education and learning but also to a person's process of individuation (Fromm, 1947/2007a). The relational holding that the child needs to be, to develop and explore the world is manifested through the body. Progressive autonomy also involves a progressive introjection of that bond, until maturity leads to knowing how to be alone (Winnicott, 1965/2011b; Bowlby, 1969/2012; Anzieu, 1998).

In children's psychotherapy during the 2020 period of lockdown, we were able to confirm that all school continuity was based on a face-to-face bond, regardless of the pedagogical skills or the content management of the adult involved. In most cases, the global emergency has required parents' commitment to assist their youngest children in the completion of their homework and the connection to virtual classes; but the most significant aspect of this commitment has been to reaffirm the emotional holding and support, a basic need of every baby, child, and adolescent (to varying degrees and in diverse ways) for their biological, emotional, cognitive, and existential development. Here the pedagogical and the psychological intersect.

In general, and without going into the psycho-pedagogical singularity of each case, children who have lost school continuity, who have become disorganized and disconnected from education, have shown deficiencies in this regard. It is not usually a problem of content transmission, which may be limited to the virtual (e.g., with the teacher through a video call or even through recorded videos or audios), but a problem of emotional, concrete, and face-to-face bond. It is worth remembering that the cognitive is nested on the affective–emotional and the intersubjective (Bowlby 1969/2012; Vigotsky, 1934/2012; Varela, 2000), as well as on the neurobiological, which at early ages is particularly stimulated through physical movement (Reloba et al., 2016). Let us remember that in best case scenarios in the pre-pandemic school, the teacher played a specific role as a face-to-face support, especially with the youngest children. When this face-to-face support was completely virtualized during the lockdown, parents had to intensify their efforts in this respect; this is manifested in greater physical, emotional, and time dedication, because in filial holding, quality without quantity is not enough.

The case of Lara, a 12-year-old girl, illustrates this. She's an only child with a father who works all day long in his successful business, even on weekends, and doesn't need to do so. Her mother, who has a part-time job and works from home, has a tendency toward anxiety and hypochondria. This corresponds to a certain narcissistic self-absorption and little predisposition to the maternal functions of holding, handling, and object presenting (Winnicott, 1986/2011a; 1965/2011b), which the father does not fulfill either; in other words, there is some difficulty in the necessary asymmetric maternal–filial (and paternal–filial) bond relatively focused on the girl (ideally, with a newborn, the focus is complete, and as they grow, there is usually a natural dosage). At the start of the lockdown, Lara stopped showing up for the school's virtual classes. In some of the interviews with the parents, they state that "she is a lazy girl" who spends all day and night on the computer playing games or watching videos, although sometimes she draws. In her therapy sessions, no cognitive difficulties were noted, but there was a great lack of motivation and disorganization with the school reality, and an important concern regarding her isolation from her friends. During her sessions, Lara states that she does not have her virtual class schedules; nor does she have the links to access them. She can only "find" the instructions for her art assignments. The links to her virtual classes and assignments are ultimately found in several forgotten e-mails in her inbox and also in an online school platform that has all the information. But what matters is that she experiences the lack of access to these resources possibly because the "emotional link" is missing. There is also chaos in her daily organization, where video games and social media interfere with hours of sleep and schoolwork (which she hardly does); the other daily activity she does of her own free will is drawing. She says she really misses meeting up with her friends, even if they play online. On the other hand, she has an aunt that attempts to help her with her schoolwork through virtual means, but this attempt fails. An attempt to help her from the therapeutic space, also virtual, to organize her habits and moments of study, and to activate online communication with her teachers also fails.

Attempts are made to work with her parents, to guide them toward greater emotional holding, and in the sessions with Lara, her preference for drawing is acknowledged and encouraged. Through her drawing, she expresses her emotional states, a creative activity that, together with the therapist's acknowledgement, seems to contribute to a general improvement in her mood. However, what really changes the school landscape is the arrival of a teacher who begins to provide face-to-face tutoring lessons. When they're done with the homework, they play volleyball for a few minutes. The following week, Lara is able to reconnect with her classes. Beyond the academic and behavioral organization that may have been facilitated by the teacher, what allows the change is the "organization" of the face-to-face bonding; this is also possibly reinforced by the guidance received by the parents, who apply the recommendations, and by the therapist's acknowledgement of Lara's interests.

Lara's case embodies the importance of the human bond during the development of subjectivity, of emotional holding and the other person's empathetic gaze. In order for the child to explore the world and learn in this interaction, they need to encounter the other. There is no virtual system of information transmission that can accomplish this. Winnicott (1986/2011a) has explained from his vast experience in children's psychotherapy that "a facilitating environment must have a human quality, not a mechanical perfection" (p. 166). Although mechanical perfection is used as a metaphor in the quote, it takes on a literal meaning today.

In the adult, the importance of the human encounter is also there, but in a different way. The person is not necessarily psychologically disorganized in cases of isolation (when the self has a sufficient integration, which occurs thanks to a previous bond). However, an adult's humanity is nourished through different forms of encounter, of shared creativity, as in the case of a love life and work life.

Perhaps because of the pandemic, society has understood the fundamental value of the figure and presence of the teacher. On their part, teachers, professors, and instructors in general have had to multiply their efforts not only to generate adapted content and corrections but also to maintain the necessary human contact. After months of pandemic, many countries have even declared teachers essential workers. This is the case in England, where Eleonor, a high school teacher and mother, lives. After months of adapting her classes to the virtual format with the new school year that began in September 2020, she had to return to face-to-face teaching and then consider a hybrid system due to the new surges in infections. These changes have meant a somewhat chaotic discontinuity, both pedagogical and in terms of Eleonor's personal and the family's well-being. She says that she enjoys and appreciates very much her face-to-face classes, where the back and forth with students takes place spontaneously, which appeals to her from the vocational point of view. She also acknowledges the comfort of having stayed at home for a while without exposure to the virus.

One of the main problems that Eleonor has encountered in the inclusion of digital resources in her classes is the overwhelming and undifferentiated amount of information on the Internet. When she conducts these searches for information and resources, she copies the links to a file. When faced with the prospect of reviewing the list of links, Eleonor feels overwhelmed because she doesn't know where to start. The task of assembling content is more extensive than in the usual format; she also needs time to provide the corrections and feedback that the institution and the parents expect from her on a regular basis to maintain and strengthen her connection with the students. She says that not only does she feel overwhelmed but that she is indeed working many more hours than before. She describes it as a work desk where every time she finishes a task an endless number of new folders with issues to solve are added.

It is worth noting two points mentioned in the UNESCO report (Futures of Education International Commission, 2020) on schools, which extends to different vital and cultural dimensions in relation to the new social and informational dynamics. The first is to revalue scientific knowledge and evidence as a criterion for organization. This is especially necessary considering the chaos of information overload and progressive dissemination of false information, which is sometimes very harmful and now growing due to the specific dynamics of social media and our uncritical participation in them. In line with philosopher Byung Chul-Han (2016/2019) and psychologist Kirk Schneider (2017/2019), the call is to refuse automatism and mechanization, and to assume our role and responsibility on a daily basis both in our face-to-face and virtual activities. The other point also mentioned in the UNESCO report, albeit implicitly, is the inclusion of an ecological perspective. From a psychological perspective, we could speak of nurturing naturalistic or ecological intelligence (Gardner, 1999/2011; Goleman, 2009). For this purpose, the conceptual contents provided by the school or other training courses are certainly useful. But, as we have already said, there is nothing like the bond and the experience of contact, which can also be provided by schools and so many other forms of learning and experiences. To understand the role of nature, our origin, and our relationship with it, it makes sense to experience it, to live it. Isolation, for example, in an apartment in the center of a large city, will probably help little in this regard. Being locked up because of the pandemic is just a hyperbole of our urban life, from the industrial revolution onward.

Finally, we may add very briefly that this crisis could be an opportunity to install the necessary paradigm shift in education that has emerged in recent decades. This shift is from a traditional objectivist, categorizing, individualistic, and fragmented education, which carries over 19th-century positivism, to a relational, multidimensional, multicultural, pluralistic and integrative planetary education, focused on navigating uncertainty and chaos within the framework of an updated humanism (Morin, 1999).

Online Work and Offline Unemployment

The pandemic has affected the labor and economic side of things in different ways, which has repercussions on the subjectivity and mental health of individuals and communities. The obvious impact in the short and medium term has been the increase in unemployment and the general drop in income. But there is also another aspect, which will possibly have a greater impact in the long term: the massification of teleworking.

The great economic losses to the world, countries, and families because of the pandemic are still incalculable. Many businesses and economic activities have been put on hold or have shut down. During the second trimester of 2020, the International Labour Organization (ILO) declared a loss of 17.3% of the world's working hours, equivalent to 495 million full-time jobs (ILO, 2020a). It also pointed to the Latin American region as the most affected, both in terms of economic recession and in loss of working hours and income (ILO, 2020b). This situation will further deepen the already existing socioeconomic inequalities in Latin America and the world. We should add that the most affected are the most precarious, less qualified workers with fewer technological resources. Meanwhile, in general, workers in the knowledge economy, professionals, and technicians have had the opportunity, and also the great challenge, to adapt to telework (if they had not already implemented it, at least in relative terms).

Both job loss and the switch to online work (which also implies a loss, although it includes gains beyond the economic) contain not only the aforementioned social, economic, and political dimensions (which we will not get into here) but also the psychological and existential. Work entails a series of human needs and quests: the provision of the means for subsistence; a way of bonding, exercising a social role, and being recognized; one's own contribution to the community; and an expression of one's own becoming and authenticity (Blustein & Guarino, 2020). We should note that in the best-case scenario work manifests the creativity of the mature individual, which allows them to reunite with the world as an interdependent being (Fromm, 2007b). It is also a space where the individual can find meaning in the realization of a creative value, where something is contributed to the world (Frankl, 1946/2013). From these explanations, we may understand how significant work is for the bio-psychosocial-spiritual whole of the person, and how its loss and precariousness poses a threat to survival, identity, socialization, and meaning. In other words, it is a mental health risk, especially with respect to chronic stress, emotional disorders (anxiety and depression), and existential anguish (of death and meaning).

Emilio is a 45-year-old Colombian man who lives in Buenos Aires with three small children and his Argentine wife. He is a very sociable person, devoted to his family and friends. Years ago, his family had enough to get by and did not go without, thanks to Emilio's job as a school minibus driver, a job he had until the start of the lockdown. When the schools closed, Emilio lost his source of income; to survive over the following months, he spent what little savings he had and looked for other jobs, but to no avail. This was compounded by a marital crisis with his wife, which was triggered by the constant cohabitation, discomfort, and complaints over the lack of basic elements of subsistence. To feed their children, he accepted bags of food from a local soup kitchen, but he experienced this as a personal failure.

Emilio starts therapy feeling a great deal of distress, on the verge of depression, and very irritable. His emotional distress is mainly linked to the emotional blow of losing his position as his family's breadwinner and the responsibility he feels for his children's needs. The structure of meaning Emilio had maintained up to that point has crumbled. It is also worth noting that this is the first time in his life that he has been unemployed, a situation that is unbearable because of his ingrained culture of work, accompanied by the idea that men should be the breadwinners in the family. He says he can't stand "being useless." This is worsened by the marital crisis with his wife, the isolation from his friends, and also his fear of catching COVID-19 because he is asthmatic and therefore an at-risk patient. He tends to overindulge in the consumption of news on television and the Internet, which increasingly demoralizes and angers him.

In the therapeutic space, we try to assist him so that he can value his help in the daily organization of the home, the meeting of basic needs, and the emotional support that he provides to his children. However, his state of anguish and irritability only improves when friends living in Spain offer him a job as a driver in Madrid. He borrows money to travel. The same week he arrives in Spain, the country, like most European countries at the end of 2020, returns to a lockdown as it faces a second wave of infections. At the time of writing, Emilio is still in Madrid. He managed to get a job at a car wash and sends money to his family, though he feels it's not enough. He's under a great deal of stress, but he feels less anguished because he understands that he is doing his best; he finds meaning in his predicament, and he also believes that there will be a way out in the short term because of his confidence in the presumed European economic stability.

Emilio's case is one of millions and reflects the psychological, social, existential, and also biological dimensions of the distress caused by the pandemic-generated unemployment crisis and job uncertainty. If Emilio were to continue with this level of stress, he would possibly be more prone to asthma attacks as well as to a further weakening of his immune system. On a global scale, it is the biological dimension that triggers the crisis in the first instance, but it is the health problems generated by the coronavirus, to the point of mortality, that slow down most economic activities.

The other major structural shock that the workforce has received during the pandemic is the massive transfer to virtuality for the jobs that will allow it. The limits of the latter definition have also been modified by the circumstances. Of course, there are some jobs that (at least for now) cannot be completed on the Internet: construction work, child or elderly care, and dental care, to name just a few.

Telework has been around for decades, and the variety of physical and mental health research that has been done over the years has always pointed to conflicting results, with different pros and cons. Flexible schedules, the ability to manage one's own time and space, the time saved from not having to commute, and the ability to focus without any distractions from co-workers have allowed a better work–life balance and even productivity; at the same time, however, we've had bad posture, a lack of communication and interactions, overwork due to undefined hours, and various physical and mental health problems (Buomprisco et al., 2021).

During the pandemic, we may again point to two paradoxical and opposing trends that are part of the same phenomenon of the virtualization of labor. In principle, one of the trends involves health risks, while the other is directed toward well-being. The first is what we may call a self-colonization of the work dimension accessed by the individual, due to the lack of boundaries and spatial–temporal limits in this 24-hour day connection. In other words, it's an invasion of work and its intersection with other areas of life. The second is the discovery of what is gained in quality of life, by not having to commute, deal with traffic, or be confined to an office, as well as the added benefit of a flexible schedule and having more time to spend with one's own family and for oneself. The ability to generate a balanced relationship with virtual work involves a relative awareness of both tendencies, and a voluntary and free construction of one's own temporal and spatial organizational structure previously provided by the office or other workspace. This requires further development of personal responsibility and awareness of one's own assessments and choices, in context and in relation to others (colleagues, family members, etc.).

One of the main problems to be solved, individually and collectively, linked to the aforementioned dynamics of social media, is the impulse toward the inauthenticity or falsehood of building an image that responds to some form of neo success on Instagram or LinkedIn, both in terms of quality of life and "significant" moments, as well as job results. Ultimately, no one escapes their own values, either by coherence or incoherence. Anguish and emptiness do not lie. In crises, these questions and contradictions emerge from the depths and become clearly evident.

Early in the pandemic, there was in many cases a kind of defensive denial and clinging to a work euphoria and hypomania, as well as an exuberance of Zoom meetings with friends and family. Over time, this gave way to weariness and hopelessness, with various consequences. In the worst-case scenario, there was job exhaustion and its most serious outcome—burnout, which increased during the pandemic in several work settings (Fox, 2020; Gewin, 2021). This can affect all workers, but especially women, who tend to bear the weight of caring for children who have had to stay at home (Thomason, 2021). Burnout involves physical and mental exhaustion, depersonalization, detachment from one's work, feeling of inefficiency, and a lack of energy even to complete small tasks (De Sousa, 2021). In the best-case scenario, the consequence of growing weary of the initial euphoria was to prioritize an authentic quality of life, giving work, relationships, and other vital aspects of life the place they deserved based on one's own values, in the exercise of one's own freedom and responsibility.

Mariel has a four-year-old son and a baby on the way. She is also the owner of an interior design and decoration company, which during the lockdown experienced a surge in business. This was both the result of the context of confinement that spurred many to make changes in their homes, as well as thanks to various communication and advertising campaigns that Mariel implemented on social media. She stayed connected with customers and suppliers through virtual channels. In light of the misfortunes so many businesses were suffering, she feels that she cannot let any opportunities pass. Clients contact her and write to her several times a day. When she tries to make space and time for her son and other non-work issues, clients complain about the lack of immediacy in her responses. For this reason, Mariel begins to respond instantly to all of her clients' messages and comments. This need for immediacy, which is characteristic of an era that does not tolerate extended processes or consideration of other people's needs, ends up generating in Mariel a strong addiction to this "contact," with its corresponding anxiety and reward in customer satisfaction messages.

In her therapeutic space, Mariel recognizes a level of distress linked to the exhaustion and anxiety of being constantly available for her clients at the expense of having sleep problems, anxiety symptoms, and the inability to feel pleasure. At the same time, Mariel says she is not willing to delegate this communication to another person, like an employee. She even believes that when her baby is born, she will be able to continue this constant communication with her clients, staying connected to her cell phone while breastfeeding, for example (she has seen friends who have done so, apparently "with no problems"). This unlimited invasion of work in all areas of Mariel's life, channeled by her cell phone—which she allows without thinking about it and reinforces by the social justification of being fully dedicated to work—leads to a kind of exploitation and emptiness. This is shown by her declaration to even be willing to relegate to second place her maternal function (which exceeds the mechanics of breastfeeding and requires attention, holding, and gaze for the healthy construction of a bond). She replaces the bond between herself and her loved ones with the connection with her customers. Likewise, the lack of limits in the use of the screen also translates into the behavior of her son, who disobeys Mariel's requests to stop playing video games, for example, and come to the dinner table.

Achieving a balance between being connected and setting limits so that virtual work, and also video games, don't invade, empty, or mix with the other aspects of life and turn it into an undifferentiated magma, is important for bio-psychosocial-spiritual health. In order to have a global, multidimensional, and reflective vision, it is necessary to get organized in context. This entails having the will and the free choice to sustain this balance in the face of the prevailing cultural tendency of unlimited connection, the very temptation to which the current technology is leading us (based on the immediate neural reward that sustains the abuse of virtual connection). This may be aggravated in times of crisis, when having a job seems to be a luxury rather than the norm.

Ezequiel is 45 years old, has two children, and has suffered a great deal of stress during several months of the pandemic because his once thriving business (event, party, and show planning) was decimated by the lockdown. At the beginning of the pandemic, Ezequiel was constantly in virtual contact with his business investors, whom he had assured a profitability that in the context of the crisis would never come. At first, he remained available and virtually communicated almost around the clock in an attempt to solve the unsolvable, constantly on the verge of burnout. Likewise, for his family there was a meaningful change in the standard of living and family culture: they no longer had three cars and had to share one; the children switched from private to public school; and they stopped spending money on anything that wasn't strictly necessary.

On a Sunday afternoon that he was spending with his family, Ezequiel blew up at one of his investors, and for the first time told him not to contact him again on weekends. This was a healthy response that helped Ezequiel become aware of his progressive discomfort and avoid burnout, which was the minimum expected outcome. From that moment on, Ezequiel set schedules and limits for his workspace. He enjoyed the time spent with his children and also outdoor sports: He returned to mountaineering (a passion that had been neglected by work). He and his wife also plan to move to a neighborhood far from the city, surrounded by greenery, to take advantage of the possibility of telecommuting. Once he is able to resolve his business situation, Ezequiel plans to pursue a smaller venture (perhaps returning to his accounting profession) and maintain a simpler life that prioritizes the well-being he is rediscovering. He says the crisis put a stop to the "whirlwind of working, earning, and spending" he had been in and allowed him to stop and ask himself if this was what he wanted from his life. It was not. He is slowly discovering what it is that he wants.

Ezequiel is an example of someone who has gone from the hypomania and confusion experienced at work at the beginning of the pandemic to prioritizing a better quality of life. Doing so calls for a clear rethinking of priorities in light of the global and individual disruption brought on by the crisis. On the other hand, both Ezequiel's and Mariel's cases also present a generalized problem that occurs when faced with the need to construct one's own limits and self-care: the reformulation of certain customs in relation to social interactions in the virtual world. The constant demand for connection and immediate response must be reviewed, as well as the idea of the rightness and wrongness of responding or not responding to messages sent at times that one defines as non-working hours.

If the person manages to set limits to this time–space undifferentiation of online work, teleworking may lead to a better quality of life because of the flexibility and the time saved and optimized. Once again, technology proves to be a tool whose functionality, specifically and in relation to the context of one's own life relies on the purpose, values, and decisions of those who use it. It undoubtedly demands a greater deployment of one's own freedom and responsibility, both the responsibility to comply with the work contract established by the parties, as well as the responsibility to healthily integrate the work into the multiple dimensions of life, leaving space and time for each of the dimensions valued by the person.

Virtual Love and Real "Overcrowding"

All social ties with family, friends, partners, colleagues, peers have been affected by the pandemic and its consequences. In this section, we will focus specifically on sexual–emotional relationships. We refer both to steady relationships and to relatively flexible relationships, as well as to occasional sexual encounters. In these bonds, we may observe two movements that have intersected our world after the pandemic: the accentuated virtualization, both in a concrete sense and in a rather paradigmatic one; and in some cases of cohabitation, a crisis unleashed by the close proximity and constant presence of the other person in isolation with us, due to latent problems that were previously hidden underneath the bustle of everyday life. In the latter case, the limit situation can lead to an encounter with the existential rawness of the bond. The (uncomfortable) comfort of the known system, despite its encounterlessness, blew up when people had to spend days, weeks, and entire months together 24/7, perhaps even after years of living together. On the other hand, the crisis and closeness may result in a strengthening of the bond. When going through the pandemic, couples may exacerbate differences and hostilities, break up, or become stronger depending on the intersection of factors such as contextual factors, individual vulnerabilities, and intersubjective resources (Pietromonaco & Overall, 2021). What is certain is that they will not be the same as before.

The first movement, that of the virtualization of sexual–emotional bonds, is a process that has been increasing since the beginning of this century but which seems to have accelerated and massified in a hegemonic way with the pandemic. In fact, during the lockdowns implemented in different countries around the world for more or less extended periods, those who were not in steady relationships have been practically forced to use social media to communicate or dating apps to meet people (even those who had never used these apps before). In many cases, the bonding has been more virtual than face to face, or even exclusively virtual. At the same time, even when taking a face-to-face form, the paradigm of virtuality tends to consolidate as a bonding pattern in terms of lightness and speed of connection and disconnection. This has been accentuated in the pandemic also by the ambivalence between the powerful impulsiveness of meeting and getting involved with a strange other and an immediately subsequent regret, influenced by fear of contagion.

The renowned sociologist Zygmunt Bauman (2003/2018) has called that relational lightness "liquid love" in the framework of "liquid modernity." He has interpreted it as the current main modality of "emotional" bonding, with a low level of engagement and an input/output view equivalent to the connection/disconnection of digital social platforms. The paradox is that people of this age are "desperate to relate" yet at the same time "wary of the state of being related" because that may "bring burdens they feel neither able nor willing to bear, and which, by that very fact may seriously limit the freedom they need to... yes, you guessed it, relate!" (Bauman, 2003/2018, p. 10). This vicious cycle, akin to a dog chasing its own tail, clearly reflects not only the current difficulty of relating sexually and emotionally and developing one's own relational existence, but also the erroneous, and we may even say pathological, concept of freedom. Freedom involves choosing, committing oneself to that which is chosen, but also enduring the anguish that this entails for that which is left aside. If we stand in front of a tree of ripe peaches without choosing one of its fruits because of the fascination generated by all of them and the defect found in each one, the peaches will end up rotting before our eyes. This very thing often happens with Tinder, Match, Happn, and other dating apps: the feeling of expectation when making contact because you "like" someone's profile, along with the compulsiveness to keep looking because "maybe there is someone better." Likewise, the dynamics of these apps, where a person is liked (not chosen) and discarded in a few seconds based on a couple of photos and phrases, as if they were a product in the supermarket, facilitates the objectification of the other and the bond that Buber calls I–It. In some sense the dynamics of these apps reflect a "commodification of the emotional bond" in a context where life in general is governed by the market, consumption, transience, and lack of time (Palumbo, 2019). Social relationships are made less complex, eroded by so much superficiality (Bonavitta, 2015). The hegemonic sociocultural paradigm focuses on the utility of immediate and specific results, on consuming life (and its pleasures) as soon as possible rather than on going through the processes and mystery of existence and the encounter between two people. Dehumanization is just a step away, as Kirk Schneider (2017/2019) points out.

Francisca is 27 years old, and her virginity has been weighing on her for a long time, so she decides to search on Tinder for men with whom to have sexual and emotional relationships. Since adolescence, she has found it difficult to connect with those she is attracted to, largely due to her own insecurities about her physical appearance. She has a group of friends who constantly talk about sex and partners, and she says she doesn't want "to be left out." After a few months of using Tinder and having the occasional failed date, she connects with a man who is a few years older. They have sex on the first date, with a great deal of alcohol involved, and she doesn't mention her virginity for fear of scaring him away. As soon as the sexual encounter is over, the man gets dressed and leaves; he never replies to Francisca again and even resorts to the kind of behavior that many today perceive as more egregious than ignoring the message and not responding: the infamous "leave on read."

There are several things that may be said about the case without going into too many clinical details about Francisca's particular vulnerabilities. On the one hand, she meets the supposed goal she had set for herself of having her first sexual encounter. The dating app achieved that much. But is this something that Francisca authentically sought? Or is it something that was imposed on her (and she allowed it to be so) by her social environment, and even maximized by the social media that visually expand the potency of what is expected from her? These questions arise when in the therapeutic space Francisca expresses all her pain and anguish over what happened, crying and needing to put words to her suffering.

Francisca felt (and also enabled) a complete neglect of the other, experienced by her as annulment in an encounter that was concretely physical but unreal in all other dimensions (including the affective–emotional one). Of course, this also could have happened without the dating app, and, in fact, has been happening since the world has been turning. The thing about the app is that it favors and exploits it (in a symbolic and concretely economic sense; it is the business of these companies). It empowers "liquid love" in that immediate, egocentric, superficial, and robotic connection/disconnection, where the human encounter does not occur and the ability to make a conquest in the blink of an eye through the virtual or face-to-face image that dazzles the conquered, is everything. In general terms, this type of technoerotic or techno-emotional device participates in contemporary isolation and individualism, feeding contacts that are functional to one's own needs and narcissistic satisfactions in the denial of relational existence. Along these lines, there are even technological developments that also seek to eliminate the "stumbling block" of the hitherto unavoidable physical encounter. LovePal, for example, simulates intercourse between two people connected to the Internet by reproducing the movements of each other's genitals through devices that connect to the computer and the body of the remote participants. Through a similar technology, Frebble simulates a handshake or caress based on actual remote movements mediated by both devices (Bonavitta, 2015). Unlike this "liquid love" that connects and disconnects with a click and is defined quantitatively according to results and utility, the human encounter is defined qualitatively in terms of processes and mystery. When the latter occurs, it may last for one night or years, but there are two people who bond as I–Thou, who listen to, talk to, and touch each other.

On the other hand, the disposition to human encounter of the two people who contact each other through these apps and social media may transcend that pre-established dynamic and end up building an I–Thou bond, its subsequent duration notwithstanding. Paradoxically, in some cases and contexts, this virtual space may even be one of the only possible spaces for this to occur.

We present a case that embodies the contrasting characteristics of this "virtualization of love." Carolina is a 63-year-old lawyer, outgoing but with few social ties; she has skin rashes that she can't stop scratching, as well as badly cracked cuticles and nails that she can't stop biting. She is depressed due to a recent separation and another separation ten years ago. She has few friends and a daughter who lives in another city. She is very much driven by her work as a lawyer specializing in administrative law, a career that subjectively sustains her. She met her ex-husband, Lucas, also a lawyer, at the firm where she was working at the time. A few years before separating from her, Lucas began a relationship with a secretary. Carolina's self-esteem was greatly affected, not only because of the separation itself and being cheated on by her husband, but also because she felt that she had been exposed in front of her co-workers at the firm. Later Carolina was in a relationship with Pedro, who suffered from persistent depressive disorder; when he went through depressive episodes, she interpreted them as being directed at her. Finally, Pedro left her, and she ended up sinking into a deep emotional slump.

When she starts therapy, Carolina is taking high doses of antidepressants, her rashes have increased, and she has almost no fingernails left. Despite her strong identification with her solid professional career, she has feelings of inadequacy and insecurity because of what she describes as relationship failures. In this regard, she reflects an insecure attachment bonding pattern, which in the therapeutic work is confirmed to have been forged in the primary bonding relationships with her mother and older brother and reinforced by her last two romantic relationships. This insecure attachment pattern sustains the hopelessness regarding her ability to have a relationship and to set self-care limits, and her high standards for any potential candidate (this will be seen later on). Her distress is centered on the obstacles she faces in her relational existence. In fact, her therapeutic objective is to overcome the suffering caused by not being in a relationship and, from there, to be able to open up to meeting people.

In short, the first thing done in the therapeutic space is to work with the unresolved grief of the first separation, enhanced by the second one. The therapist's unconditional acceptance and empathy toward Carolina is of great importance. The question then arises as to where she might meet people. Work takes up most of her time, and she has almost no social life. After a few unsuccessful attempts to reconnect with old friends, the therapist suggests using social media and dating apps. Carolina's first reaction is to scoff at the idea, considering it impossible. She has never done it before and doesn't even know how it works. The therapist tells her that if what she's tried so far hasn't worked for her, it's a great reason to try something new. So, Carolina starts using Tinder and other dating apps. From that moment on, a new social world opens up for her; she had never before been in contact with so many strangers showing an interest in her. This leads her to articulate a better version of herself, which creates new mental maps of her self-image. It improves her mood. The sessions no longer focus on her ex-husband but on the new experiences Carolina has on Tinder; she also spontaneously takes things with humor.

While in this case there are positive effects, the dynamic that dating apps sustain by default is also present: the ease of objectifying the other and the "liquidity" of the bond. There are men who even before meeting her suddenly stop talking to her after days of fervent chatting, others who upon seeing her make up an excuse and leave. There are also those who, after what had seemed like a good first date or sexual encounter, stop replying to her messages and, what is sometimes worse for her, also "leave her on read." From time to time, Carolina tends to go back to her list of failures and feel victimized, that she is available to everyone and no one is available to her. However, before long she also catches herself doing the same with other people. In the therapeutic space, this role reversal, of victim–victimizer, is treated with humor (although very seriously), where in these I–It bonds Carolina may be on either side of the equation. The role of victim she was stuck in loses weightiness. Her biases and long list of requirements are also discussed, as well as the feeling that she's shopping for products in a supermarket, which the dating apps replicate. For example, when she is contacted by men who are older than she is or who possess physical characteristics that she doesn't like (i.e., they are overweight or bald), Carolina is outraged and asks how these men "have the gall" to talk to her. By observing that she, too, has done what she doesn't want others doing to her, there is an awareness that she is not simply a victim of fate; she may choose to continue in the same victim–victimizer, I–It dynamic, or choose another.

Carolina begins what we might call her dating app adventure in 2019 and continues it through the 2020 pandemic. In the middle of that year, after several disappointments she suffered or brought on herself and helped her to put aside the role of "the one who's dumped," she meets Hector, a man with whom she talks for hours and with whom she seems to share views on several issues. However, at first, she is still drawn to the thrill of the app and its endless provision of new options, because "there could always be someone better"; the dopamine generated by the reward circuit with this expectation is reproduced to the extent that the person keeps looking and looking, with the result that she doesn't find what she's "looking for." As explained by Bauman (2003/2018), there are people who seek a bond but choose not to bond in order to be available in case of a possible future bond. However, little by little, Carolina chooses to make room for meeting and getting to know Hector in a real and human way, getting out of the vicious cycle of "there could be someone better." They talk a lot, virtually and in person, and throughout the day she begins to think of things to tell him. In this conversation and encounter with the other, she finds herself and the vitality of her experience. Finally, an I–Thou bond is built, and a "we," where one takes care of the other and one chooses the other. They spend every weekend together and take turns staying at each other's place. Hector helps her with her skin problems: He accompanies her to the dermatologist, buys and applies creams, and she helps him lose weight with healthy food. In this way, a space of secure attachment is built in this "we," whose face-to-face emotional bond is integrated and nourished by the virtual channel that was the initial point of contact and continues to be used on a daily basis with other apps as a means of communication. Regardless of the duration of Hector and Carolina's relationship, it is a real human encounter in the sense of authentic presence, recognition of the other, and openness to intersubjectivity.

It is interesting to note that with her former husband, Carolina suffered because she had no one to talk to; she was emotionally and, therefore, humanly alone, even though she was physically accompanied. This incoherence is what generates pathology. This same incoherence is present in so many couples who live together in physical presence but are absent in their (bio-psychosocial-spiritual) being. The image that comes to mind is the person who does not respond to or look at their partner while the latter is talking to them, or who disappears into the cell phone when getting into bed with the other next to them; what's more, it's the person who needs to watch pornographic movies before having sex with their partner. Cell phones, social media, and the virtualization of life facilitate and are a factor in sustaining this situation of absent presence, although they are not necessarily the cause. The feeling of loneliness caused by a partner who is physically present but humanly absent is related to an ambiguous, unresolved loss because it is a confusing type of loss (Perel & Miller, 2020).

On the other hand, the sudden and constant proximity brought about by the pandemic due to the lockdown and the 24 hours a day spent in the same physical space, has catalyzed latent problems in some cohabiting couples. In the case of the absent presence, for example, the situation reduced the possibility of hiding this. The sudden and constant proximity, experienced in some critical cases as a kind of symbolic "overcrowding" of the couple (we are not referring here to the actual overcrowding that occurs in specific vulnerable social contexts), is the other issue that we have observed in the psychological clinic. In the crisis, the relational existence is unveiled and imposes itself on the couples, no longer in the guise of their daily routine. It raises the possibility of examining it, reviewing it, and rethinking it in its evolution. Because the crisis is a rupture, which inevitably changes the structure built so far, for a couple this may involve a separation, an improvement in the relationship, or the consolidation of discomfort and dysfunctionality.

The case of Mateo and Carmen may shed some light on this. Mateo is a 33-year-old photographer, and Carmen is a 39-year-old publicist. They have three children and have been in a relationship for over a decade when the crisis strikes. For a year or two, there has been a certain uneasiness between the two, which they have not been able to put into words. Daily photography work for a government agency takes up most of Mateo's week, and he returns home late at night; on weekends, he usually has plans with his friends. Carmen coordinates between work and taking care of her children and complains that Mateo is not present enough in the family's daily life, reminding him he was the one who wanted to have kids in the first place. Mateo complains about Carmen's low sex drive and her reluctance to engage in sexual encounters, with the added complication that she suffers from frequent urinary infections.

It is worth mentioning that Carmen has grown a lot in her professional career and has a different emotional maturity than Mateo, who has not yet made much progress professionally; and although he says he is working on it, he feels frustrated about not displaying his talent. Carmen is the one who supports the family financially and emotionally, while also supporting Mateo when he has bouts of insecurity. In short, Carmen is more of a mother than a partner. She positions herself in the maternal role and thus participates in this asymmetrical dynamic that has not allowed for a joint project, but she is also angry that Mateo does not fulfill the symmetrical role of partner.

When the lockdown occurs, Carmen and Mateo find themselves in the same house 24/7. The discomfort and anger cannot be avoided. Finally, they talk and try to make sense of what is happening to them. They understand that there is a lot of affection between them but no real "we" or a common project to support it. In the midst of the pandemic, they decide to split up. In this context, Mateo rediscovers his fatherhood by taking care of his children in the middle of the week, both in its dimension of responsibility and emotional support as well as in playful interaction. In time, he finds more profitable work as a photographer and starts planning an exhibit of his own. In short, Mateo grows in terms of autonomy and individuation; the dynamics of the bond he had with Carmen sustained his immaturity. In Fromm's (2007b) terms, Mateo finds himself alone when faced with his own decisions, losing the constant shelter of the structure provided by another and not seeking an equivalent one; that is, the situation of separation confronts him with his freedom and individuation. His development in this regard also affects his relationship with others (the relationship with his children clearly symbolizes this).

On her part, Carmen went through a lot of sadness over the separation, which resurfaces from time to time. She no longer feels constant anger, no longer has urinary tract infections, and is getting to know someone with whom, if the relationship progresses, there seems to be a possibility of building a more symmetrical bond.

The context of the pandemic and the constant proximity between Mateo and Carmen generated a kind of symbolic "overcrowding" that evidenced the inauthenticity of the current "we" despite the real affection that existed between them. In other cases of the millions of couples who have faced this crisis, the "we" may have been reformulated and reinforced, or the dysfunctional pattern may have been reproduced, which is dysfunctional for all family members.

What About the Body We Are and the Nature That Surrounds Us?

The limitless virtualization of experience contains the risk of disembodiment of life. Can there be experience without body? At the same time, technology seems to be taking on a certain form of corporeal extension as a means of finding new ways of experiencing life. How can technology be included to broaden the embodied human experience without restricting or instrumentalizing it? In a joint interview published in early 2021 in the journal of the Latin American Association of Existential Psychotherapy, Yaqui Martínez Robles and Ramiro Gómez Salas, two renowned psychologists in this school of thought, put forward contrasting, though perhaps complementary, ideas in this regard.

Martínez Robles states that although the body seems less present,

> from the screen, I can notice certain things about your face that I would not be able to see otherwise. I have less body, but more face. Electronic devices are instruments, but paradoxically speaking, they are also extensions of my body. For example, the phone becomes an extension of my memory with my contacts and stored data; of my eyes when I zoom in or take pictures... Through the computer I can transmit my voice and image and receive yours. It is true that sometimes we instrumentalize ourselves a little, but we can also embody and humanize technology, through the subjective experience of it. (Segafredo, 2021, p. 40)

On his part, Gómez Salas states that

virtuality is a super-reality that allows us to converse and see each other but does not allow the space for intimate encounters. We've been through thousands of years of biological evolution in which the gaze, the smell, the movement, the temperature are constituted in the subjective experience of the presence of another. Virtuality is often seen as a problem of skills, ignoring the ontological impact. There is a beautiful description by Octavio Paz of the romantic encounter. He says that the body of the beloved has valleys, peaks, plains, and depths that one never finishes exploring. By contrast, recently, a Peruvian TV report on how to spend Valentine's Day featured a journalist in a sex shop: she showed a ring that the man could put on his penis and that his partner could make vibrate whenever they wanted, from their cell phone. Technology will try to give the person what reality does not. But the ring and the game they can play while miles apart will never replace the person in the flesh. We don't have a body; we are a body. (Segafredo, 2021, p. 40)

The arguments presented by Martínez Robles and Gómez Salas clearly reflect opportunities and risks in the current paradoxical virtualization of life with respect to our corporeality. On the one hand, there is a significant relinquishment of our corporeality, and, on the other hand, there are new possible experiences of it. It may be useful to take a step back and put these reflections and our embodied experience into perspective.

Given the problematic tendency of virtualization to disembody human experience, it is worth remembering that the modern Cartesian paradigm nestled in the Judeo-Christian tradition has sustained for centuries the soul–flesh or mind–body split, with multiple dualistic ramifications such as idea–emotion or rationality–intuition, which are still very present in contemporary sociocultural discourse and in medical and psychological clinical practices. But there are also several integrative paradigms in circulation that recognize a bio-psychosocial-spiritual gestalt in the human experience of being. These are perspectives where the mind is not circumscribed to the brain, like software to hardware (the computational metaphor is not insufficient, but inadequate) but is "fully embodied or bodily inscribed, enveloped in the world" (Varela et al., 1991/2011, p. 240).

A current advance in biomedical science that is beginning to understand mind–body integration is the discovery of the relative autonomy of the nervous system that covers the intestine, in which we find 80% of the neurotransmitters that are the cause and consequence of mood. Likewise, the emergence of disciplines such as psychoneuroimmunoendocrinology also bear scientific testimony to this perspective. In the philosophical dimension, authors such as Merleau Ponty describe the corporeality of the phenomenological experience of the individual, and spiritual traditions such as Buddhism propose exercises of meditation and full presence that rediscover the embodiment of the mind in an alignment of thought and sensory experience (Varela et al., 1991/2011). Whether or not we recognize and take advantage of it, the mind is inseparable from the body and is reciprocally co-determined with the world and others in a corporeal, emotional, cognitive, and existential-based bonding (which occurs as a whole and not in fragments). To describe this conceptualization of consciously experienced embodied gestalt, Kirk Schneider (2017/2019) speaks of a "whole bodily being" (p. 80) and even the meaning that each person may construct as an "embodied meaning" and of the vital commitment that this involves as "a whole-bodied orientation towards life" (Schneider, 2008/2015, pp. 80–81).

An unbalanced use of virtuality could reinforce the paradigmatic and false split of modernity and even lead to a confusing distance from the corporeal dimension, which would basically be distancing us from ourselves. This involves connecting to virtuality and disconnecting from one's own body and its link with others and the world. However, the body always exists and is modified based on the process experienced. Those who spend their days in front of a screen without complementing this time with other activities will tend to suffer from muscular atrophy in addition to other medical problems caused by a sedentary lifestyle, as well as a worsening of their vision. To focus only on these physical–functional issues would be to neglect the embodied presence of all human dimensions such as the emotional, cognitive, and existential.

In children's psychotherapy, we have noticed an unexpected phenomenon that points to this. The extreme virtualization of life during the pandemic has led many children and adolescents of the new digital generations, surprisingly and spontaneously, to ask for physical contact with friends and family. It is not enough to play and socialize online with the other; they need to do it in corporeal presence. This is related to the explanations given for the need for physical–emotional bonding support for learning, and also to the significance of corporeal presence in loving (sexual–emotional) interaction. We have already seen in the section on "virtual love" the role that presence has played both in the construction of the "we" between Carolina and Hector and in the awareness of the non-existence of the "we" between Mateo and Carmen. In the section on virtual education, we reported how only children with physical–emotional bonding and holding have had school continuity during the pandemic.

The origin of the corporeality of human experience lies in its conception: The fetus comes to be in the body of another. The baby builds its identity in the physical–emotional contact with the mother, father, or other caregiver. When the latter does not happen, even when fed and washed, the baby goes into an anaclitic depression, and then death, as explained by Reneé Spitz. On the other hand, when this physical–emotional contact occurs, skin to skin, between mother–child (caregiver–individual receiving care), I–Thou—where the mother's I (Thou) empathizes and believes physically, emotionally, cognitively, and existentially in the child's potential Thou (I)—the natural miracle of the construction of subjectivity occurs. In describing this bonding process, Didier Anzieu (1998), expert on psychoanalysis of intersubjective bonds, recognizes the concept of Skin–Ego. The I–Thou encounter and the consequent (and causative) subjectivity are primordially skin to skin. The interface of the person with the other and the world has a corporeal foundation. For this reason, we may also say that, in general, presence facilitates the I–Thou human encounter, although it does not ensure or monopolize it.

At the origin of affection and in its actualization, we find the body, but also the possibility of conversing with and fully encountering the other: There is a being here together with the other in intention, attention, feelings, and assertive communication from the body (Reynoso, 2017). In this regard, we may say that the virtuality that comes closest to corporeal presence is the video call, which allows synchronous communication where, in the best-case scenario, the voice and gestures of the other person's face are clearly perceived; this is where the extension of the senses proposed by Martínez Robles becomes present. Quite different is the case of the extreme mediatization and symbolization implied by a text message, for example, with its lack of corporeality; hence the emergence of emoticons, which are very useful although limited by their rigidity and universality. The meaning deciphered by the receiver of the message (in its sensory texture a rather unidirectional and unlinked communication) will allow the more or less accurate recreation of the corporeal dimension, such as tone and emotion.

On the other hand, the body also contains our existential reality: potentialities and limits to our capacity to experience the world and life, to transform them creatively and freely, as well as the inexorability of their finiteness. The existential mystery of life and death takes place in the body. In short, human existence (which includes the mind) is embodied. The disembodiment of experience, which is proposed by perspectives that raise technology as an end in itself, means dehumanization. An extreme example is the transhumanist movement, which seeks continuity of mind without body, immortality, and absolute control of the variables of existence in an attempt to turn the human being into a machine. This would involve an (illusory) pre-programing of life, which means ignoring the inexorability and richness of its mystery, as well as annulling the creative becoming of the person, their authenticity, their freedom, and responsibility in context. As Kirk Schneider (2017/2019) explains in his essay on the subject, what is at risk is the humanity in humanity.

Virtuality is not the problem, as long as it is primarily a means to the human ends of existential unfolding in terms of becoming, freedom, and bonding. When this is the case, it becomes a powerful humanistic resource. But if virtuality becomes the end and the person the means, mental health problems arise (with a dehumanizing base), some of which we will present in the next chapter.

On the other hand, the paradox is that virtuality contains a healing potential with respect to an individual's subjective and, specifically, physical isolation. It may contribute to building specific intermediate spaces with transitional and potential characteristics (Winnicott, 1971/2015), to help transcend obstacles, internal and external, in the existential unfolding of the person (in their different levels of freedom) and bringing the experience back to the body. The obvious contemporary example is the contact we have been able to maintain during the pandemic with our loved ones and significant others, in a continuity and actualization of our relational existence. It has functioned as a bridge between the impossibility of meeting in person and the future real encounter that we long for. Although it is not entirely that encounter, in a way it is: hence its transitional nature, which is cultural and also personal in terms of what each person brings to create that "encounter."

On the other hand, there are several therapeutic applications of virtual tools, specially designed and used by cognitive–behavioral psychotherapy, which help to lift roadblocks at different levels. One of these may be the psychoeducational use of virtual representations of areas of the brain and body activated during times of emotional distress, called Brain Training Tools (Scherb & Durao, 2017). These virtual representations could function as an intermediate space between symptomatic self-absorption, the capacity for self-distancing or metacognition, and a more conscious relationship with one's own embodied subjective experience. From the cognitive understanding of the physiological dynamics of one's own distress, this self-observation may help to understand one's own suffering and to consciously experience it, with a possible alleviation of rumination (and the consequent reduction of distress) and strengthening of coping resources.

Another therapeutic application is the contribution of virtual reality to the progressive exposure to an object or situation connected to a phobia, so that it loses its weightiness as such. The virtual re-creation of the real situation allows an intermediate approach with transitional characteristics, which, at the same time, is and is not an approach to the object or situation. Technological progress as a cultural experience allows the "as if" that the person then ends up enabling and co-constructing. There is something illusory and playful that at the same time re-creates the represented reality and helps to face it in person at a later time. The latter is fundamental: that the virtual may function as a preliminary step to the encounter of the person with concrete reality, as the embodied existence that it is. Something similar may happen with the bonding approach through social media and dating apps for someone very introverted who initially finds the intensity of the face-to-face encounter hard to bear. Virtuality could facilitate a more progressive and smoother bonding, with subsequent face-to-face presence.

Returning to Winnicott's (1971/2015) initial concept that is at the root of these reflections, the transitional object makes sense in the child's development and well-being to the extent that its protagonism (or significance) is diluted and not eternalized. It may remain as a reminder of the child's maturation process and of their acceptance of their separation from their mother and their consolidation as an individual. Something similar happens with the virtual when it plays an intermediate role in the approach to a more complete reality. The problem arises if the virtual crystallizes its protagonism at the expense of the protagonism of the true and embodied self in its interaction with others and the world (Von Boetticher, 2016). At the same time, we may reflect on virtuality as a contemporary cultural creation and experience and, therefore, as a transitional phenomenon and potential space that is part of the intermediate zone (between the internal and external worlds) of adult life, so it is always and will always be in interaction with spatial reality and our subjective becoming. The important thing, once again, is to be clear about its nature as a means and not as an end. This is where we can take up Martínez Robles' idea regarding technology and virtualization as an extension of the body; from our point of view, this will enhance human development if we think and practice it as a transitional, intermediate space that does not replace the face-to-face encounter with the other and the world but complements it and expands it.

Achieving the humanistic use of virtual technology to complement face-to-face encounters requires a balanced and conscious plan. It is also important to understand the difference between adult and child use. As the person develops subjectively, virtuality may be sustained for a longer period of time in relation and in reference to an already experienced corporeality—just as the capacity to be alone can be sustained in relation to a previously experienced secure emotional bond.

On the other hand, we must be aware that virtuality can neurologically activate the same circuits as the activity previously experienced in person, even if at a lower intensity. This is related to the capacity of a specific group of neurons called "mirror neurons," which activate sensorimotor areas of the brain as if the body had performed this action (Damasio, 2003/2014). On the other hand, it indicates that what is done on a virtual plane has its physiological correlate, as does every human experience (a thought, for example, is the cause and consequence of biochemical processes). This again reinforces the importance of the use of virtuality because its content enriches or impoverishes subjectively. While watching soccer virtually is not exactly the same as playing it in person, it activates (to a greater or lesser extent) some of the same neural circuits. Complementing some virtual visualizations with face-to-face training may be useful for an athlete.

Likewise, a similar neural dynamic explains the emotional connection and empathy between people, which occurs from the perception of the other's emotional experience in expressions and gestures. Through an "as-if body loop" (Damasio, 2003/2014, pp.132–133), this process re-creates an equivalent corporeal–emotional state in the one who has perceived the other, both in person and in some virtual formats such as a photo or video call. There are several studies that confirm neural changes equivalent to the emotion of the other at the mere sight of pictures of faces, for example. This neurological explanation of empathy, where the emotionality of the other is reflected in oneself, could be thought of as the physiological substratum of the Buberian I–Thou of our relational existence. It illustrates the already mentioned qualitative difference between a virtual encounter by video call and an exchange by text message, which has fewer elements to activate the "as-if body loop" of empathy. If the level of description of the text is deep and heartfelt (as can happen with a literary text where we empathize with the feelings of the character, thanks to the writer's expressive and symbolic capacity), it would still require a greater effort and commitment on the part of the person who receives it.

Since the crisis of in-person presence brought on by the pandemic, it has also been noted that the empathy generated by virtual channels produces a greater exhaustion with respect to its face-to-face dynamics (Reynoso, 2020). This is experienced both by psychologists, whose assistance is based on empathy, and by people who have used virtuality to arrange various daily meetings. This may occur because the virtual channel presents less stimuli and gestural and expressive variables than the other because of an excess of one's own expressions and constant rearrangement in front of one's own image on the screen. In addition, this can occur because of a certain defensive stress reaction to the delay of feedback caused by technical obstacles. Empathic emotional recreation would thus be more difficult and could possibly require more effort. In fact, some preliminary studies show a greater empathic attitude on the part of therapists who use video calls compared to those who only practice face to face (Durao, 2017), possibly as a consequence of a greater effort and intentionality of the former to recreate the empathic connection of the face-to-face encounter and compensate for the lack of corporeality (Hirsch & Durao, 2020).

On the other hand, it is interesting to analyze the sudden emotional intimacy that is achieved with acquaintances and strangers in collective meetings through virtual platforms such as Zoom or Meet, which might not exist in face-to-face meetings. We are referring, for example, to school and university graduation ceremonies, which have had to be held in virtual format due to lockdowns and social distancing. The possibility of seeing on screen and in real time the faces of several of the participants and their particular emotionality achieves a sudden and surprising closeness. There is an emotional content, very present in the face of the other, which appears in the close-ups that are interspersed in meetings like the ones mentioned above. Moments of intimacy also emerge in that strange terrain where the boundaries between public and private social roles and personal lives are blurred. Another difference of this dynamic with in-person presence could be the immediacy of the passage from distance to intimacy, and vice versa. There are processes of in-person presence that do not occur, and thus the durability of states and encounters does not fully materialize, either. We could say that this intimacy and closeness have authenticity at the moment they occur but an authenticity in a liquid state (Bauman, 2003/2018), which mutates in an instant.

Another influence of technology on subjectivity is its growing use as an extension of cognitive functions—for example, memory (in gigabytes or teras) or visually–spatially (with GPS and its directions). This technological delegation and extension of our psychological functions could transform human physiology in the long term. This also occurs with the sensory side of things, as pointed out by psychologist Martínez Robles (Segafredo, 2021), who sees in the camera an extension of the eye, and in the speakers, an extension of the ear.

Therefore, conscious decisions about what to channel and what not to delegate to technology will be critical. To give an example that we have already mentioned in some detail, we cannot delegate to technology the maternal emotional bonding care of a baby or a child, as happens daily with the collective hypnosis of the screen to which millions of parents give their young children.

There are situations and experiences that demand the total presence of the person, including the body (and not as a technological extension, more or less transitional). Another example at the opposite end of the welcoming process that occurs with the subjectivity of the baby that arrives a little at a time, is that of the farewell. When a loved one dies, the farewell to the body, carried out with the body itself and in a collective encounter that remembers the departed, allows the mourning process to take place. The impossibility of doing so may accentuate denial and generate pathological problems of complicated grief. During the pandemic, this has occurred in thousands of cases around the world, both in deaths due to COVID-19 (Aguiar et al., 2020), as well as those from other causes. Virtual channeling is not enough in these situations either, although it is certainly better than no contact at all.

Javier, a speech therapist in his forties, has been in a relationship for a year and a half with Elisa, a woman in her thirties. She is Spanish, and he is Argentinean, and they live together in Buenos Aires, where they met a few months after Elisa came to work for a well-known multinational company. Javier only knows Elisa's family by video call. They had planned to travel to Madrid in April 2020 to visit Elisa's parents and siblings but were unable to do so because of the lockdown. They had also planned to get married in mid-2020 in Buenos Aires, a wedding that would be attended by their family and friends. In the midst of the pandemic, Manuela, Elisa's mother, is diagnosed with laryngeal cancer. She undergoes surgery and during her recovery, thanks to his profession as a speech therapist, Javier helps her with various exercises to recover the use of her vocal cords through daily video calls. He recounts this experience in therapy, with much enthusiasm and affection for his mother-in-law. Manuela improves quite a bit despite her limited vocal situation. During the exchange, because of the process of illness and recovery that they go through together, they generate a significant emotional bond, even though they have never met in person. However, there are two planes of indirect corporeality in that bond. On the one hand, Javier is Elisa's partner, who is genetically and emotionally linked to the mother who raised her. On the other hand, the virtual channel creates a real physical modification. What they do together takes shape in the improvement of Manuela's vocal cord use and speech.

At the same time, and despite the lockdown, Elisa and Javier decide to get married in an intimate ceremony limited to two or three attendants due to the health emergency. They make an appointment at city hall many months in advance. Then, despite her improvement after surgery, Manuela suffers a serious relapse and ends up dying suddenly two days before Javier and Elisa's wedding date. They are both distraught over the news. Javier feels a lot of frustration, both for the help provided that did not prevent her tragic end, as well as for not being able to meet his mother-in-law in person. Elisa tries to travel but even with urgent arrangements to be included in a repatriation flight, she would not make it to her mother's wake or burial. There is also uncertainty about the possibility of her returning to Buenos Aires. Elisa's relatives insist that she should stay in Argentina and also that she should not cancel her wedding, which might be postponed indefinitely. Javier and Elisa get married three days after Manuela's death, the day after the funeral.

In therapy, Javier reveals discomfort and confusion over the emotional ambivalence he feels. Both he and Elisa were sad about Manuela's death and happy about the wedding. Within hours, they seemed to leave one state and enter into another one. A few days later, however, Elisa is hit with a great deal of confusion and bewilderment.

Just as they were not physically present at Manuela's funeral, neither did they experience the physical presence of their family and friends at the wedding. There is something that does not end up happening in one ceremony but that fundamentally does happen in the other. Both are present in the bonding commitment that is celebrated at the wedding, which is a process that they go through and will continue to go through daily in their own bodies and together with the other's body. However, mourning is a process that lets you say goodbye to someone in its emotional–cognitive–existential embodied totality (as a bio-psychosocial-spiritual being); that is, it demands accepting the end of the embodied presence of the loved one. To do so, physical closeness with the departed and with loved ones is important. This makes it possible to remember the deceased together and also to reconstruct the new reality, with the absence and the particular legacy of the loved one. If this farewell does not occur, there is a risk that the denial phase, present in all mourning, will be prolonged (Kübler-Ross & Kessler, 2005/2018) and that the wound of loss won't follow its course of healing, and thus generate psychopathology.

Both of these variables, the impossibility of seeing the body and sharing the farewell ritual with others, are risk factors for pathological grief (Vedia Domingo, 2016). This is even more so in the case of the death of a mother or maternal figure. We take up Anzieu's (1998) concept of "Skin–Ego" as subjectivity constructed and under construction, physically and emotionally held by the bond with the significant other. It is from the Skin–Ego, the concrete ground of the I–Thou bond, that one's own person emerges, and it is from the Skin–Ego that the significant other is let go. In other words, from one's own corporeal I, one says goodbye to the significant and corporeal Thou. This conceptually explains the experience of feeling that when a loved one dies something within us dies, too.

Javier and Elisa wonder if they had lived in the same place as Manuela and had been present at the wake, if they would still have gotten married. They don't think so. This may well be true. Virtuality favors the sudden passage from one state to another, the liquidity of states. And when it takes on the character of a unique channel, it is insufficient to process vital moments fully and deeply (as in the case of maternity, mourning, romantic love). It is, in fact, very helpful as a complementary channel.

Being able to accept and be present in a life situation engages the body. From cognitive science, we speak of full presence as a state that involves being here and now as a body–mind alignment, in coherence with our embodied mind (Varela, 2000; Varela et al., 1991/2011). Existential psychology also speaks of presence, in line with the authenticity of being. And authentic experience requires corporeality (Schneider, 2017/2019, 2008/2015), because as we register it, we have the indication that we exist in relation to ourselves, to others, and to the world. At the same time, in the perception of technology as a possible sensorial and neuronal extension, as stated by Martínez Robles as cited in Segafredo, 2021), the question of whether virtuality is taking on a more concrete corporeality, a material dimension, resonates with us. If that were the case, how would it happen? In short, how would we choose to make it happen? This may be, for example, with the awareness of the central place of our physical body and our humanity, or not.

When speaking of corporeality and materiality as the embodiment of conscious life, we need to make at least a brief reference to the nature from which we come. In his elaboration on life, neurobiologist and neurophenomenologist Francisco Varela (2000) explains that the human being contains a developed nesting of cognitive capacities of other terrestrial life forms whose emergence is the consciousness and the self but whose roots go back to unicellular organisms. Our embodied mind is, therefore, an expression of our earthly nature, a nature which, from the Judeo-Christian tradition up to the modern paradigm (with positivism as an extreme), we have subdued and isolated from us. The process of differentiation from nature that the human being has gone through has had its meaning, as has the process of individuation of a person with respect to others and the world.

However, completing the process of development and realization involves becoming reunited to the world and to one's own autonomy, in a bond of interdependence, as proposed by Eric Fromm (2007b). We can take up this analogy to consider that humanity, present in the collective us and also in the us contained in each person, has the vocation to be linked to the Earth in an improved interdependence, the denial of which would endanger the planet and, therefore, human existence. Thinkers of the stature of Edgar Morin (2020) have understood this global political, social, economic, ecological, cultural mega-crisis, triggered by the pandemic but latent for decades, as an inexorable call to our planetary identity and to a new form of planetary humanism that includes all living beings. This is a possibility and a hope, perhaps the only realistic one, since both our human dignity (which is an existential vocation) and our collective and, therefore, individual survival depend on it. "We had never been so physically confined as during confinement and never so open to earthly destiny. We are condemned to reflect on our lives, on our relationship with the world and on the world itself" (Morin, 2020, p. 17).

Not only have thinkers called for the awakening of awareness and transformation, but so also have countless artists, such as Roger Waters in a video posted on social media: "Going back to our normal lives is not an option. We need to get back to something that is far much better than what normal was before this virus. Because what the virus has shown us is just how disgusting that normality is." Ordinary people around the world have participated in this spirit of reflection and transformation during the pandemic, with countless messages on social media. The outcome of this is still a mystery, but as we mentioned in Chapter 2, the global limit situation has generated an inevitable existential reflection in most of us. And virtuality has undoubtedly helped to spread it.

The paradox lies in the fact that isolation due to the danger of contagion from the other, which has allowed introspection, also reflects our inexorable bond with the other in good and evil, as well as with other living beings—both because of the alleged contagion from animals to humans, as well as the respite in production and consumption that has revitalized nature. The bond is evident in the many images of vegetation and animals that returned to their places of origin in a demonstration of the incredible regenerative capacity of the ecosystem. So it was with the crystal-clear waters, the fish and dolphins in the canals of Venice. This image has traveled the world through social media and has become a symbol of how the ecosystem can regenerate if we allow it to. At the same time, the bond with nature and ecological sensitivity require physical contact; affection and consideration for ecology, and living beings require some level of corporeality, as does the human relationship. In order to be real, every bond requires at least a prior corporeal base. From this footprint, it can then have more or less complementarity and derive nourishment from the virtual base. We can also say that corporeality needs to be updated from time to time.

As in any bond, there is a dyad that feeds on each other. Neuroscience confirms that children's contact with nature is good and necessary for their mood and emotional health, as explained by neuropsychologist Carina Castro Fumero in an interview on the Instagram account Tanconectados (2020). We can also say that the physical contact of children (and adults) with animals and plants, with gardens, trees, rivers, dogs, horses, birds, and the like contributes to their vital richness, to their relationship with nature and to their planetary identity. Feeling the warm and rough tree bark and listening to the rustling of the leaves as they are caressed by the wind while hugging a tree; witnessing the company of a dog that won't leave your side on a long walk; hearing the hum of the hummingbird as it is suspended in the air while it extracts the pollen, and so many other experiences generate and regenerate our bond with nature. The environment needs it, but fundamentally we need it as the planetary beings that we are. We are called to recognize ourselves as such, symbolically and corporeally, in order to be in a more integrated and complete way.

Chapter 4

Our Distress and Our Existential Resources

The sociocultural, psychological, and existential processes that have unfolded since the start of the pandemic are multiple, complex, and still evolving as we write these words. Isolation and medical and economic chaos have wreaked havoc on mental health. Like any limit situation, this one contains psychopathological risks but also potential for growth and transformation. The seeds of both horizons are present, both collectively and individually. In this critical context, the virtualization of life has also been installed, with the rapid spread of new psychological problems related to the excessive use of technology. It is a problem that has progressed for the past two decades but has grown exponentially since the pandemic. The sociocultural and even economic roots of these problems make the situation more complex. For example, the addiction to constant connection is also based on the social naturalization of "living" almost exclusively through cell phones; and on the business side, we have the various tech companies that make money with the user's attention span, the prime example being social media.

Reflecting on mental health in this context of crisis and extreme technologization and virtualization, as well as activating the nutrition and the building of resources to cope with it, is an urgent matter. In light of this urgency, we present a few trends (among others) that we have noticed at the crossroads between clinical psychology and today's society, particularly in relation to uncertainty and the relationship with ourselves, with the world, and with others.

This chapter does not intend to respond to a specific or exhaustive psychopathological systematization but rather to present certain mental health problems that are affected by the dynamic critical and sociocultural context in which we live. Our perspective has a humanistic and integrative anthropological base and includes several psychological conceptions, especially those related to emotional bonds and cognitive and existential aspects. It also contains dimensional vocation; that is, it understands that there are nuances in shared traits whose imbalance toward one extreme or the other may involve a pathology. It seeks to guide the reader, who may be more or less specialized, with respect to forms of distress and also potentialities that emerge from an extremely virtualized culture in the context of the uncertainty and existential crisis unleashed by the pandemic. Likewise, this analysis intends to highlight the application of existential–spiritual human faculties: acceptance, meaning, creativity, and bonding, both when it comes to facing psychopathological risks and taking advantage of the possibilities of transformation and human development contained in the global limit situation and in the personal tragedies that may have occurred.

These are two sides of the same process, occurring at the same time; the distress generated by a crisis is not overcome by the relief of returning to the starting point (this would be a painkiller and a short-term illusion), but by the realization and relief that come as a result of further human development. What Frankl (1946/2013) calls finding meaning in inevitable suffering and Schneider (2008/2015) considers as deepening the exercise of one's freedom within the limits of circumstances, Fromm (2007b) and Winnicott (1986/2011a) posit as creative living, and Kabat-Zinn (1990/2016) understands as an attitude of embracing total catastrophe, where through acceptance and full presence, awareness and life experience are expanded.

In short, we will describe a few trends in terms of virtualization, uncertainty, and radical isolation whose excesses may lead to significant distress and form roadblocks for an individual's humanity with respect to their becoming, their relational existence, and their freedom in context; this in turn involves problems in the relationship with the uncertainty of life, with oneself, with the world, and with others. We will analyze anxiety and depression, narcissism and inauthenticity, addiction to being connected and inability to be present, and cyberbullying and social (self-)marginalization in their current manifestations. And just as in one extreme they become specific clinical problems, they speak to us of sociocultural trends of discomfort that are worth addressing with an overall vision.

On the other hand, both a balanced virtualization and a transformation of the crisis into personal and collective development could be both cause and consequence of the strengthening of those fundamental human characteristics and manifestations (becoming, bonding, and freedom) that make for a more authentic existence. With this in mind, we will propose some general lines of intervention (to be contextualized in each particular situation and case) for the nurturing and practice of existential–spiritual resources.

A Pandemic of Anxiety and Depression

Several studies and meta-analyses confirm the massive increase in stress, anxiety, depression, and irritability (and specific related issues such as post-traumatic stress and complicated grief) in several countries since the pandemic began (Kontoangelos et al., 2020; Salari et al., 2020). Benchmark data from a global meta-analysis indicate that by the first half of 2020, 33% of the general population was feeling anxiety, while depression was present in 28% (Luo et al., 2020). These emotional problems affected to a greater extent people infected with COVID-19 or with previous health conditions. In the general population, the main risk factor was living in contexts or situations of socioeconomic vulnerability, as has been the case of the millions of newly unemployed in the world. Other risk factors reported are isolation, having a high likelihood of infection, and spending a great deal of time consuming information about the pandemic, while protective factors include having sufficient medical resources and reliable, up-to-date health information, as well as taking precautionary measures (Luo et al., 2020). Uncertainty and certainty thus provided risk or protection, respectively.

In several countries, like Argentina and the United States, a significant increase in symptoms of depression was recorded in 2020. In the case of the United States, a comparison with the pre-pandemic situation indicates a threefold increase (Ettman et al., 2020). In the Argentine study, conducted during the extended national lockdown, sadness, lower energy, and increased alcohol consumption were recorded especially among young people; also symptoms of depression were prevalent among those who had greater socioeconomic vulnerability, with job loss and low income (Alomo et al., 2020). In Germany, there was a significant increase in anxiety symptoms, with almost half of the population affected, and psychological distress, with over 60% affected (Bäuerle et al., 2020). In relation to anxiety, fear of the coronavirus has been one of its pillars, to the point that there were specialized analysts who spoke of coronaphobia (Asmundson & Taylor, 2020). This possibly fueled xenophobia (which literally means fear of the stranger), especially in the early months of the pandemic with respect to the Chinese population in different parts of the world. For example, in the United States, there was an increase in racist attacks on people of Asian descent during 2020 (BBC News Mundo, 2021).

Since the beginning of the COVID-19 outbreak in China, the viral pandemic has been accompanied by a psycho-emotional pandemic, reconfirming that body and mind are the same totality. The paradox is that the discomfort generated by fear of the virus or by stress when faced with its consequences, increases cortisol (stress hormone) levels, whose chronic presence lowers immune defenses and therefore weakens the body, which is thus more vulnerable to COVID-19. Given this context, the World Health Organization (2020) called on the various countries of the international community to strengthen their mental health policies and systems. The WHO explained that "bereavement, isolation, loss of income and fear are triggering mental health conditions or exacerbating existing ones." Beyond the coronavirus itself, what lies at the core of the emotional malaise of this era?

One possible answer is uncertainty. An Argentine study on the feelings among Latin Americans triggered by the pandemic recorded uncertainty as the most prevalent, present in 65% of the population, almost doubling the 36% of anxiety (Signorelli et al., 2020). Beyond the study itself and its sample of 429 people, anyone can see from their own experience, as well as that of relatives and their own community, that uncertainty has fed the fear of contagion; the fear regarding the economic sustenance and survival of their own family and the country; the sadness over the disruption to daily, social, and working life and to one's own personal plans; as well as a possible "return to normality"— as if at this point, they still think there is a chance of returning to pre-pandemic life. Although in 2021, there are places and moments where, thanks to vaccination and other massive measures, there seems to be a glimpse of a certain "normality" without masks or lockdowns (which still come and go with the arrival of new variants), there is something that has changed within us.

Uncertainty in and of itself influences physical survival, the continuity of roles and social bonds, and existential projects. But today uncertainty affects not only individuals and families but also communities, countries, and, fundamentally, the whole of humanity in its biological, psychological, social (political, cultural, and economic), and existential multidimensionality. This multiplies the power of the individual limit situation, which is in turn collective. A basic characteristic of the limit situation is the rupture of the structure of certainties. And although there have been months of improvement in several countries (lower number of cases, reopening of activities, and lifting of restrictions), a month later the crisis returns. This has been the case with the different waves and variants in Europe and South America, for example. Uncertainty returns again and again; at the time of writing, it seems to be here to stay for a long time.

This shatters the supposed era of certainty, where technology and science have advanced in unimaginable ways in the field of production and in medicine and communication, with both very good and negative results for humanity. This is the case of the cultural pretense of absolute control of natural resources, as well as of our bodies, emotions, and bonds: one pill to sleep, another to have sex, another to not be sad; one app to have thousands of "friends," another to avoid the commitment of making a call, another to know how to breathe. In this context, a microscopic organism has reminded us that existence is not linear, that existence happens and spills over into our plans, that there are no apps or pills for everything. Likewise, the uncertainty of existence also reminds us that nothing is set in stone, that the world, society, and each of us are constantly in motion, and we co-construct ourselves at the intersection between our creative freedom and the circumstances that present themselves to us. Ultimately, what arises in the face of this uncertainty of the pandemic limit situation, which returns again and again, is the question of meaning: the one that we've had so far and the one that has to be processed in each new context. The only certainty is uncertainty and the creative posture in the face of it: freedom in circumstance, as the Kierkegaardian synthesis of finite and infinite that is human existence.

Except for those who have put in place mechanisms of denial, or who immediately found a concrete meaning in the pandemic itself because of some particular situation (as may be the case with vocationally present health professionals, journalists, or other essential workers), each of us has had to process some kind of more or less significant loss. The more significant the loss, the greater the psychopathological risks of suffering emotional disorders, and the greater the potential for transformation and subjective growth. This must be contextualized in the individual's mental structure, with its resources (the capacity for resilience) and vulnerabilities. The grieving process par excellence is mourning the death of a loved one, and its scholar, psychiatrist Elizabeth Kübler-Ross (Kübler-Ross & Kessler, 2005/2018), has left us a vast knowledge in this regard: Various stages are experienced that overlap without fixed linearity but with a starting point in denial and a point of arrival in acceptance. In between, there are moments of anger, negotiation, and sadness, stages that must be gone through for the healthy processing of the loss.

The same occurs in the face of any significant loss or profound change (Conangla, 2002): the death of a loved one, the loss of a relationship after a breakup, the space of cultural identity in the case of a move, a social and family role in the case of someone who suddenly loses an important job, health in someone who is diagnosed with a serious illness, a meaning in the case of any important project cut short by an unexpected situation, and daily security in the face of an epidemic or other massive crises. In each person, community, country, and continent, there will be different losses and particular changes to be processed. We can say, however, that on a human scale we are experiencing a great loss of certainty that sustained (and was sustained by) our pre-pandemic way of life, and we will have to wait and see if we manage to process it collectively. There are large groups that go back and forth from denial, anger or irritability and negotiation, as well as sadness; at the same time, an individual process in each person composes them. Although we talk about the collective and point out its importance, we operate from a particular subjectivity, which is of course interdependent.

The line between an emotional disorder and logical emotional distress in a crisis is very fine. When going through a crisis where a loss must be processed, there can be depression symptoms such as sadness, hopelessness, a sense of emptiness, and loss of meaning; there are also symptoms of anxiety such as excessive worry and fear of the future, irritability, and difficulty concentrating. (American Psychiatric Association, 2016; Conangla, 2002; Kübler-Ross & Kessler, 2005/2018). These emotional circumstances are part of the process, stops to be made. The important thing is for the person not to become trapped or fragmented in the emotional instability to the point that it becomes chronic and a disorder (e.g., in the form of complicated grief) either because of the fear of what is to come, in the case of anxiety disorder, or because of the certainty that something negative has been installed and there is no longer anything to aim for, as occurs in depression (Mazzulla & Gómez, 2011). Groups have more complex and variable dynamics than individuals; however, they can also stagnate in states of serious collective malaise such as community passivity in the face of painful events.

There are several reasons why a psycho–emotional pandemic is spreading in the world today along with that of COVID-19: The poor processing of the significant losses contained in the crisis is one of them, as well as the widespread and poorly supported feeling of uncertainty. The cognitive concept of rumination is also related to both. Anxiety and depression are sustained and maintained by rumination. In short, this is a mental struggle against the situation one is living, which generates a vicious cognitive cycle that adds suffering to the inevitable pain of existence and stops one from being and developing actively in the present. In rumination, there is useless complaining and confrontation of the distance between the real situation and the supposed ideal situation, even though the events have already occurred and are unchangeable (when they are modifiable, rumination is fixed on the problem and goes beyond the planning and resolution of the possible change). It occurs when the human mental mode of doing, focused on achieving goals, "volunteers for a job it can't do" (Segal et al., 2013/2015, p. 123).

Contemporary global culture is based on the modality of doing, which has nothing wrong with it in itself because it allows planning and achieving objectives. However, when doing completely takes over mental attention, as has occurred on a massive scale in recent history, it tends to consolidate pathological rumination. This problem is linked to the contemporary cultural and individual obsession with immediate results to the detriment of processes and in favor of an empty materialistic obsession with success; it is also linked with the control and certainty of life, whose extreme manifestation is the transhumanism that seeks eternal youth, immortality, and control of all variables in science and technology. These illusory pretensions are undone in the inevitable mystery of existence (Schneider, 2017/2019). The pandemic is both an event and a metaphor that reveals life's uncertain events, in the face of which the pretense of certainty is shattered with such clarity that the cultural matrix that sustained it could probably be transformed. Also because the excess of control, certainty, and short-term obsession with success is embodied by a productive power structure in crisis, unsustainable from the socio-economic, environmental, psycho–emotional and existential points of view (Morin, 2020).

The transformation of the collective humanity and of the humanity contained in each person can be a realistic hope, even if it is not the only possibility. A substance abuser may overdose and continue to use after recovering from that limit situation; likewise, our culture, addicted to illusions of certainty, may continue to sustain them after a massive and global COVID vaccination. We can't be sure yet, and the process of change—both that which occurs in favor of transformation and that which occurs to leave things more or less the same—will take place over the years. On our part, we intend to contribute to the course of humanist transformation, which we consider to be that of greater human wealth and well-being.

That said, how does one respond to emotional disorders in the critical pandemic and post-pandemic context? From a global biopsychosocial-spiritual vision of the human being—where the physical, the cognitive–behavioral, and the emotional–relational will always play a key role—we can say that the existential–spiritual dimension is now taking center stage. Beyond the specific case in question, it is possible to reflect on certain generalities, which, as such, must be contextualized in each situation; they involve the existential–spiritual faculties that we have already described: encounter, acceptance, meaning, and creativity.

Emotional bonding and psychoeducation are two basic elements to take into account in the face of the emotional distress caused by an individual limit situation arising from this collective crisis, so that the person or group may recognize and express the process they are going through in a supportive bonding space. In other words, within a bonding context that offers holding there is validation of what one is going through, an emotional validation in the encounter as well as self-awareness, through clear information regarding the processing of the losses and the collective and individual circumstances of uncertainty. In this way, it is possible to differentiate between the inevitable pain of the crisis and the added suffering of rumination. For example, if a person is sad or angry about what has been lost, let them feel it and not add mental suffering by fighting against that sadness or anger. In this same vein, the bonding space of trust must allow the emotional expression of the discomfort that the person is experiencing.

Psychotherapy is of course the ideal place for this; however, there may be others depending on the possibilities and circumstantial needs. We are relational beings, and in this pandemic more than ever we need the validation of the other through encounter. The bond contains the self when it's faced with the disorganization brought on by the crisis, and awareness of the process one is going through helps the person accept the inevitable circumstances. This awareness contributes to the disarticulation of rumination and to the presence of the person in the process they are going through. Likewise, we may add information about the neurophysiological process that occurs during the emotional discomfort related to the situational crisis being experienced. For example, we may explain how anxiety is linked to the body's natural response to dangerous situations, which triggers the sympathetic nervous system and may be made chronic through recurrent activation even without the presence of real danger. We could also explain which neural circuits are involved in the excessive worry of the kind of anxiety that is pathological and the neurotransmitters that trigger them, such as serotonin and noradrenaline; we may also describe the feeling of fear that hyperactivates the amygdala, the orbitofrontal cortex, and the anterior cingulate cortex (Eguiluz & Segarra, 2017). Neurobiological psychoeducation has been shown to aid self-distancing and metacognition, which in itself lowers the level of anxiety and may positively modify circuit activations (Scherb & Durao, 2017). Knowing both the emotional path of one's own process, as well as its physiological activation and the interrelation between both, may reinforce awareness, acceptance, and the coping with the discomfort and the crisis one is going through. Perhaps this is the reason for the great success of several popular books that explain brain function and basic mental processes.

As a consequence of the lockdown, Jimena, with previous tendencies toward anxiety and obsessive behaviors, has lost the possibility to travel and undergo the fertility treatment she has been waiting and preparing for (emotionally and physically) after several attempts to get pregnant and a miscarriage. She envisions the treatment postponed by the lockdown as a last chance in what she considers a race against time to have a child at 39. Fear, sadness, and worry over having lost her chance to be a mother trigger her anxiety. As the weeks go by in isolation, anxiety generalizes and expands to family, work, and social life, manifesting as fear of losing her clients as a freelance designer because in view of the decrease in economic activity, she would not be good enough to compete with the best, let alone with so much anxiety; also as fear of losing her partner, a businessman who travels often and continues to do so because he sells essential products; and fear of being alone.

Within the framework of the therapeutic space, a detailed neurobiological and psychological explanation of the anxious activation of stress and fear even when faced with stimuli that pose no threat, together with the explanation of her attacks (and her loss, not necessarily permanent, but loss nonetheless) in the context of the pandemic, facilitate a certain distance from symptomatic self-absorption and a comprehensive acceptance of what is happening to her. The symptoms start to disappear. At least part of the discomfort is reduced, and the ruminative struggle against sadness and fear decreases. This metacognition about what is happening helps her accept the emotions she feels. This is especially so regarding the topic of motherhood, but also in her work and with her partner she stops being paralyzed by fear; she still feels fear, but at least now she identifies, accepts, and lives with it. She also manages to work therapeutically with bonding patterns and unresolved issues with her older sister. In the context of the global crisis and her own crisis, and even when faced with the uncertainty of motherhood, she rediscovers small activities that bring her joy and fulfillment at times: seeing her friends, first online, and then, when possible, in person; knitting with them and exchanging knitting techniques and designs; hiking in the mountains near the city where she lives.

As in Jimena's case, the comprehensive acceptance of the situation may be nourished by this information (from the subjective crisis and the neuroendocrine response) that is processed cognitively within the framework of the supportive emotional bond and its validation. Likewise, this may be incorporated even more existentially and corporeally through the practice of full presence in its different attitudinal and meditative, formal and informal formats. This practice works on the cultivation of the modality of being, with attention on the present as it happens and without judging it, as opposed to imbalance with respect to the hegemonic modality of doing that is linked to success. The practice of mindfulness can take place in a therapeutic setting or in other preventive and wellness-promoting spaces. There are several programs, which we will not get into here, run by several of the works cited in this regard that may be accessed by anyone. Whether through the specific practice of mindfulness or through other modalities, exercising the freedom to understand and actively accept the critical situation is a key aspect to deactivating part of the mechanisms that sustain emotional disorders such as rumination.

Comprehensive, conscious, and active acceptance also facilitates other human existential faculties, such as meaning in inevitable suffering. Giving meaning to what happens during a crisis and finding a potential "what for" involves engaging with one's own becoming and exercising one's freedom in context. At the same time, as Viktor Frankl (1946/1986) explained, finding a purpose in the inevitable suffering of a limit situation alleviates to some extent the suffering of that situation itself. Mental attention is less focused on the incongruence between the real and ideal situation so that rumination is attenuated and attention does not remain fixed on the inevitable pain. The focus is on realizing the significant purpose found in a positive and healthy way of doing. This refers to the cognitive–behavioral dimension of this resource.

Frankl (1978/2014) has systematized a technique that works with the described dynamics, but with a bond and extension toward the existential dimension: Dereflection involves finding a meaning valued by the person that allows them to leave the symptomatic self-absorption in the deployment of self-transcendence. However, if the person is in the midst of dealing with a loss, care must be taken to ensure that they do not withdraw completely from the process that they are going through. The course of action is to find a "what for" without ceasing to go through the emotional process. This "what for" may help to unblock possible dysfunctional stagnations that have slowed down the process, such as the currently widespread emotional disorders. On the other hand, the realization of meaning in a crisis involves a subjective growth that takes advantage of the existential possibility in the limit situation; it transforms the context of discomfort into development of the self and deepening of authenticity. In the framework of a psychotherapeutic space, the existential Socratic dialogue may help to undertake this search. In this case, the therapist asks questions, more or less direct or indirect, about the potential "what for" contained in what is happening, with the intention of opening the door to the person's own answers about their vital commitment. The timing of this intervention is fundamental. In general, the denial and anger stage of grieving would not be appropriate for this type of dialogue. Whereas the stage of sadness, once the acute emotional flood has passed, may be a good opportunity, particularly if the person is spontaneously motivated to do so.

Committing oneself to one's own becoming involves finding meaning also (and especially) in situations of crisis, and vice versa. As psychoanalyst Fernández Mouján (1999) explains, the life crisis (unexpected or developmental) involves a field of possibility and creation. At that moment, our responsibility regarding our way of being-in-the-world becomes evident. That is to say, an implicit sense in every crisis is to deepen our subjective development, to strengthen and enrich our self in the recognition and unfolding of our authenticity based on what we really value. This is the possibility of being more coherent with ourselves and growing in our relationship with others and the world through what we can generate and appreciate.

Marcelo owns a financial consulting firm with his brothers, inherited from his father, who left the business a few years ago but is still very much present on a symbolic level. For some time now, Marcelo has been unhappy at work. He does not find motivation in the growth achieved by the consulting firm; this discomfort has been spreading to other dimensions of his life. Marcelo only feels good sporadically when he manages to escape to a friend's house in the country, where he likes to run for miles and miles, which he says helps him not to think. Most of the firm's clients are from his father's time, and even new ones are often linked to the trust that the father has built up, both occupationally and socially (among other social activities he has been actively involved in the development of a well-known tennis club). When the pandemic hits, the firm's activity drops abruptly for a few weeks, then resumes and even goes up. During the first strict lockdown, Marcelo spends a lot of time with his family, his wife and children, as well as with himself. On days when he can't even go out to play sports, he feels a deep slump in his mood. By contrast, the lockdown leads him to value the possibility of spending more time with his children. Likewise, moments of reflection awaken in him a feeling that nothing of what he has done at work or socially (he is part of the board of directors of the same tennis club) is his own. Although the consulting firm is doing well in the critical pandemic context, the work is increasingly demotivating.

Marcelo begins therapy with a great deal of anger and irritability with no apparent cause, until in one session he realizes that he did not see (as he interprets it) that he has lived in his father's shadow for decades. He decides to make a complete life change, to build something he can feel authentically his own, but does not know where to start. After going through his history and reflecting on his conflicts, motivations, and values, the anger dissipates and gives way to clarity about his possibilities for the future. He decides to sell his share of the financial firm to his brothers (he feels reassured that he is doing so at a good time for the company), and with his wife's and his children's approval, he moves the family to another province, where Marcelo starts his own small farming business and does financial consulting for other larger farming activities. At the start of this new adventure, he says he feels vertigo, but he has also taken a weight off his shoulders and has renewed energy. He claims that he is finally learning to believe in himself.

To complete the process of transforming the crisis into subjective development, we need to add creation to the acceptance and significance of the limit situation. In other words, this is the creative action that may be expressed in every person as an eminently human characteristic, and which is an excellent manifestation of the true self or one's authentic being (according to Winnicott or the existentialists, respectively). The great creative action that the crisis calls for involves re-creating oneself based on the potentiality and courage to rethink who I am and what I value. The shattering of the structures of certainty generates a field of possibility and deployment of one's own creativity, like few others. Fernández Mouján's concept of life crisis may be applied today both on an individual and collective scale, and at the intersection:

> It's a crisis because it pulls us out of deterministic structures that give us a sense of security, and because it forces us to face the danger of the unknown (...) which gives us the opportunity to produce something unprecedented. It's a life crisis because this transformation consists of the creation of something nascent in every life cycle or traumatic situation experienced. (Fernández Mouján, 1999, pp. 15–16)

To follow the logical line demanded by the argument, up to this point we have talked about creativity from the existential dimension, as in the re-creation of life projects in the cases of Marcelo or Marta (the latter presented in Chapter Two: she re-created her forgotten vocation and activity as a teacher after her family suffered a crisis caused by the loss of her husband's job). As for the specific emotional discomfort in the context of processing a loss or a situation of psychopathological stagnation, creatively reprocessing this emotion can be very useful. For example, the transformation of that emotion through an explicitly artistic activity such as writing, painting, and music may help someone go through and process that discomfort from an active and vital posture. Artistic quality is not measured, but the process of human transformation is appreciated. In contrast to the result-oriented approach that the hegemonic culture of certainty and control tends to impose, here the focus is on the process, which constitutes a synthesis between the modality of being and healthy modality of doing. Someone might want to write, for example, a poem about what is happening to them emotionally; but what matters is the value of the process of this writing and its subjective richness, not the literary "value" of the poem.

This is what Jimena, for example, does through knitting, where she adds a bonding aspect to the alchemy of the creative process as she carries out the activity together with her friends. In Lara's case, presented in the previous chapter, she is a girl with a natural predisposition to draw, and she expresses her emotional states in her drawings and paintings. There is a remarkable clinical relief of Lara's discomfort in this creative activity, which emerges as a form of reprocessing and generation of a transitional space that allow her internal world and the external world, the situation prior to the loss and the loss, discomfort and realization, the traumatic and the vital to intersect. Both Jimena's and Lara's examples show spontaneous artistic and creative activities; however, even in people who don't do anything explicitly creative on a daily basis, in moments of crisis and emotional distress artistic activities close to the person's personality can be sought in order to transform those emotions. On the other hand, physical activity may also be a way to transform the emotions that generate distress through the creativity of the body and its movements.

Artistic or physical creative activities are somehow a smaller scale expression of the existential alchemy of the crisis that can generate the re-creation of the life project, which also provides relief from suffering. This relief is a side effect of human subjective growth, which can be facilitated by working with acceptance, meaning, and creativity. All this occurs within the framework of the encounter and its emotional and existential bond, whether through a therapeutic relationship or other significant human I–Thou relationships. This bonding emotional encounter is necessary in every crisis and in overall human becoming, but in this pandemic of lockdowns and social distancing, it has even greater significance.

It can be difficult to work on these resources when you don't go to therapy with a mental health professional, but it is even more difficult when you are unaware of your own distress. In the context of the ups and downs of the global health crisis caused by COVID-19, which, through new variants, lockdowns, and economic crises reactivate the limit situation and deepen uncertainty and depressive and anxious disorders, a chronic emotional state that does not reach clinical pathological manifestations also takes hold. Some call it "languishing." Languishing includes a chronic and subtle sense of stagnation and emptiness, as if one were aimlessly passing the hours of the day observing life "through a foggy windshield," as psychologist Adam Grant (2021) put it in an article published in the *New York Times.* This is the general result of the chronification of isolation, of the pandemic and its fierce uncertainty, of the comings and goings that have broken the illusion of a return to "normality." This is a state of mind that does not become depression or anxiety but that may keep us individually and collectively dull, alien to life purposes and self-realization and very prone to future psychopathologies.

Languishing seems to be the result of this kind of blurred and permanent limit situation, where the longing for daily life and minimum permanence of plans and certainties is broken with each new surge and restriction of activities. And so, a kind of collective and subtle learned helplessness arises: The person stops responding to the crisis and the adverse circumstances they are experiencing because of a progressive loss of confidence in their ability to cope. Initiative is giving way to passivity in the face of what is happening. Although passivity is not total (as in learned helplessness and severe depression), it colonizes the person.

The focus on specific and daily practices of meaning and creativity, self-awareness, presence, and bonding exchange, as well as simple daily organization and routine, are of utmost importance in this strange and swampy territory, which corrodes a person's entire existence. Undoubtedly, one of the current urgent challenges is the development of prevention plans and interventions, both formal and informal, to register, address, and transcend this languishing in various settings at the educational, occupational, and community levels.

Narcissism and Inauthenticity in the Digital Society

The acceleration of the inclusion of online digital technology in our daily lives has generated a very powerful expression of some issues that have already been taking root in society in recent years regarding the relationship with oneself (which necessarily involves our relationship with others). Among others, these issues include narcissism and the construction of a false self that certain virtual dynamics seem to facilitate and feed.

Several studies have noted the general increase of narcissism in the young population over the last few decades of the 20th century and the first decade of the current century, to the point of considering that in Western societies there could be a "narcissism epidemic" underway (Twenge et al., 2008, 2012; Vater et al., 2018). This corresponds with theoretical essays by different contemporary thinkers, such as Lipovetsky (1983/2014) and Byung-Chul Han (2016/2019).

On the other hand, several psychological studies correlate narcissism with the increased amount of time on social media (up to problematic and dependent use), posting of selfies, status updates, and different forms of self-promotion (Moon et al., 2016; Halpern & Valenzuela, 2016; Andreassen et al., 2017; Sukhdeep et al., 2018). Some researchers even delved deeper and registered the relevance of the crossover between narcissism and low self-esteem in the persistence of behaviors like taking selfies (March & McBean, 2018). Likewise, an aestheticization of the self has been witnessed in social media (Marra e Rosa et al., 2016), seen as exposing aspects of one's identity considered positive in the eyes of others while concealing and censoring more vulnerable aspects. Social media has become part of the daily process of constructing one's own identity. This is especially so in the case of adolescents, who still lack a structural backbone in this aspect and require greater recognition and acceptance than adults. The hyperexposure and hyperstimulation of digital society seem to multiply demands, in the face of which many teenagers sacrifice their own authenticity (Del Prete & Redon Pantoja, 2020). Extreme cases of self-censorship and putting makeup on one's virtual self may lead to the construction of a false self on social media and associated psychological problems (Gil-Or et al., 2015). A relationship is also empirically registered between the construction of a virtual false self, the posting and reposting of self-promotional content, and the levels of narcissism that modulate this attitude (Turel & Gil-Or, 2019).

However, no matter how blocked it may be (and perhaps even more so for this reason), the search for one's own authenticity is constantly present in our experience. Its lack thereof, multiplied by the sociocultural dynamics analyzed in this chapter, produces deep discomfort. And it reflects one of the major psychological conflicts of our time. Sherry Turkle (2011/2017), a psychologist specializing in technology, puts it in these terms: "I believe that in our culture of simulation, the notion of authenticity is for us what sex was for the Victorians: threat and obsession, taboo and fascination" (p. 4). Likewise, we'll see how narcissism in the adult is in some way a false turn of that failed search for one's own spontaneous gesture.

We have mentioned in previous chapters the analysis of contemporary thinkers like Byung-Chul Han (2016/2019) and Zygmunt Bauman (2003/2018) regarding how social media, dating apps, and other virtual platforms propitiate a narcissistic individualism on the rise: the liquidity of bonds, the monologue, and the increasing narrowness of our worlds, which algorithms reduce us in order to facilitate new forms of digital consumption. What is automatically recommended to us by the different social, search, and content platforms is increasingly similar to ourselves: movies, shows, videos, video games, "friends," matches. Likewise, on Tinder we "like" or discard people based on a couple of photos and phrases, as if we were window shopping in a sexual–emotional mall; on Facebook we have thousands of "friends" who may not be that at all; on Instagram the icon is the selfie and its addictive search for "likes," regardless of whether we bond with the person who "likes" our content; on Tik Tok we binge on short and gimmicky videos tailored to our tastes. On a general level, we idolize the projected and desired success for oneself: careers, moments, and spectacular places (rarely real) where what counts is the result and not the process. We post about ourselves to get "likes" that endorse and validate us to keep posting more about ourselves. Byung-Chul Han puts it this way (2016/2019): "Digital interconnection facilitates exhibit spaces for the ego, in which one advertises mostly oneself. Today, the Internet is nothing more than a resonance chamber for the isolated ego" (p. 141).

There is depersonalization and impoverishment in reducing the world to one's own reflection. We all talk but no one listens. The response is emptiness. And this emptiness is installed as a sensation and leads to the psycho-emotional problems mentioned in the previous section: One goes very quickly from narcissism to depression, for example. Meanwhile, technology companies make money with this personalized consumerism, in which each person is a bubble that consumes itself and also constructs (falsely) itself based on the expository logic of the social medium in question. It consumes itself and lends itself to being consumed. This is where narcissism intersects with the inauthenticity of one's own profile, creating a kind of false self, which then leads to emotional problems and may have a deep impact on people's subjectivity. Feeling real, authentic, and true to oneself, recognizing oneself as present and the protagonist of one's own existence is possibly one of the main indicators of health and well-being, as stated by Winnicott (1986/2011a), Rogers (1951/1989), Yalom (1980/2015), and existentialists in general.

To exemplify the problem, we will return to the case of Juan (presented in Chapter Two), a young man suffering from a high level of anxiety, who for some time had the plan to become an Instagram "lifestyle influencer," inspired by the celebrities he follows. Even before the pandemic, Juan was constantly and repeatedly posting photos of his daily life on his profile. During the first lockdown and the euphoria of being online and on social media, the activity on his Instagram account increased. He uploaded photos of most of the things he did for his 3,000 followers. Everyday activities were meant to be recorded by the camera and posted on his profile in order to get as many "likes" as possible. Each photo went through several rehearsals, a meticulous selection, and editing, with priority given to showing off his muscles, the setting, his artificial smile, and the occasional silly face to show his fun and cool side, along with training, eating, picking outfits to wear, or discovering some wonderful new place. The more he posted, the higher the anticipation and the more often he checked (very common in obsessive tendencies) for "likes," which were never enough and were ultimately met with greater anxiety and emptiness. To fill this void, he would post some more, and he was caught in a vicious cycle of dependence and anxiety.

One day, in a therapy session, Juan realized that this apparent exposure of himself, this "photoshopped life," was not even his: "This guy who wants to look like an advertising model is not me." This revelation was triggered by a relationship with a younger cousin with whom he lived and played with during the lockdown (one of the only activities he didn't do for the camera). Sometimes his cousin missed his mother, and Juan discovered in this child's feelings something powerfully genuine. Juan described it as missing someone from within, not for the camera, like when he said in some of his posts that he missed his followers, most of whom were not his friends and many of whom he hadn't even met.

On his Instagram, Juan, like so many others, objectifies others without realizing it by turning them into an (illusory) means to inflate his self-esteem, a bubble that can burst in seconds. But Juan also becomes an object for others. He constructs a false Juan (an inauthentic self), who never says how he really feels and what he really thinks but only what he thinks will get him "likes"; he avoids showing himself in a sincere way. This takes place among other variables because the dynamics of this social network, when dealing with a narcissistic tendency, enables the fake Juan more than the real one. This deepens the feeling of emptiness and the difficulty in relating to others and to oneself. These are issues that Juan is currently working on in his therapy, which paradoxically is virtual. Because, as we argue throughout this essay, virtuality is not predefined; in fact, just as it can foster dehumanizing (and therefore unhealthy) dynamics, it can be a powerful tool and conduit for human encounter if it is used conscientiously and responsibly to that end.

At the same time, dosage is important. Who can deny the usefulness of entertainment platform algorithms recommending shows that are similar to others we have liked? Who would think that uploading a photo of an achievement or a fun moment to a social media app and the satisfaction of others celebrating it with their "likes" and comments is going to generate narcissistic discomfort? Who can deny that keeping in touch through social media with a friend who lives far away helps maintain the relationship and allows two people to stay up to date on each other's lives? The complementarity between face-to-face and virtual social life can enrich the interactional experience. The problem arises in the many cases similar to Juan's, where life is imprisoned in the narrow world of our profile. When this is the case, it invariably ends up being a false profile (in addition to addictive internet consumption), which favors an inauthentic self. Even beyond the features that a specific platform and social network stimulate, can someone be only what they expose in a profile?

In the same dimensional line of doses and imbalances, neither narcissism nor the construction of a false self is in itself pathological. Let's take a step back, to explain this and fully comprehend what it is that generates distress in narcissism and inauthenticity, which by default are facilitated by certain virtual dynamics when platforms are not used in a balanced way.

Several psychologists who have studied narcissism, such as Freud, Kohut, and Winnicott, each in their own way recognize it as a central manifestation of a child's subjectivity (Freud would speak of state) during emotional development, which, however, in a persistent and dominant adult display represents emotional immaturity and fragility of subjectivity, with pathological forms. From a relational and development of the self perspective, narcissism in the child requires the empathy of the adult caregiver, the mother, the father, or whoever fulfills that role (according to Kohut, although to a lesser extent, there are narcissistic needs throughout life also in the healthy individual that require a renewed response from the other). The maternal caregiver responds and adapts with "ordinary devotion" (in Winnicott's words) to the needs and illusions of omnipotence of that subjectivity in the process of becoming, which, from the holding and narcissistic gratification found in that bond, can focus on itself in order to know, structure, and integrate itself during these stages of dependence (Mitchell, 1988/2018; Winnicott, 1986/2011a, 1965/2011b, 1971/2015; Kohut, 1977/1980). From a process of sufficient individuation, which also involves a progressive disillusionment, transformation and transcendence of that narcissism (which continues to appear, albeit not needing center stage anymore or to be taken so seriously), the person will reach self-awareness and the ability to bond and exchange with the other in a symmetrical way.

This process is necessary for the expression and unfolding of the true self, which begins in the baby's spontaneous gesture and unfolds in a subjectivity that feels real, coherent, and capable of expressing its creativity and generating the authentic human I–Thou encounter. This is also so for creative expression (in love, work, art, and other forms), through which the individual gathers with others and the world, from his own autonomy and individuality, to constitute the healthy interdependence that a humanist and democratic society needs, as Fromm (2007b, 1947/2007a) would say.

When the child does not find holding, support, and empathic reflection in their mother or caregiver, two related processes occur that may be problematic and sources of discomfort. On the one hand, the child's narcissism is not transformed because in the absence of the ordinary devoted mother, it has never even occurred; it has not been allowed. This may manifest itself in adulthood through various forms of illusionary overvaluation—the fundamental problem outlined by Freud's pioneering *On Narcissism: An Introduction* (1914/1993)—such as persistence of illusions of one's own grandiosity, extreme idealizations of others whom one feels attracted to or admires and would like to emulate, and symbiotic illusions of fusion (Mitchell, 1988/2018). On the other hand, the lack of empathy and the maternal reflection of one's own spontaneous gesture (which is omnipotent in childhood narcissism and the basis of a sufficiently integrated personality in the adult) lead to the defensive assembly of a false self, which hegemonizes the way of being, hides that spontaneous gesture, and is built upon the foundation of the child's submission to the significant other. They will copy the other, do what they think the other wants, or attract their attention (Winnicott, 1965/2011; Mitchell, 1988/2018).

The false self is not in itself pathological. In its fair measure, it fulfills a social function in some inauthentic expressions and gestures that are performed based on what is expected of one by the shared cultural exterior, necessary for coexistence and good manners in society. The problem occurs when it completely dominates the person. It arises as a defense and a protection for the true self against an environment that has not allowed it to be, but it could end up hiding the true self so deeply that it completely disconnects the person from their spontaneous gesture. "The False Self, however well set up, lacks something, and that something is the essential central element of creative originality" (Winnicott, 1965/2011b, p. 198). What arises in the person is emptiness, the feeling of not being, which in the most serious cases may lead to very risky situations, including suicide (Winnicott, 1965/2011b; Kohut, 1977/1980).

The basis of these processes occurs during childhood, but the integration of subjectivity continues throughout life and may be challenged and strengthened when the person is faced with life difficulties and crises. In Juan's particular case, his primary relationships had historically been emotionally lacking, which could be related to a kind of emotional fragility and difficulties in bonding. In other words, there is a previous vulnerability that is activated and accentuated in the egocentric and inauthentic dynamics (by default) found in the social network. To this, we may add a tendency toward narcissism and a false self that was already present in Juan that finds in the social network the perfect channel of expression. There is no linear causality, but feedback loops. Although he channels some of his narcissistic illusions, Juan feels that the profile he put together is not really his own. In this case, it is as if the use of virtuality multiplies the environmental demands that may subject a person in the construction of a false expansive self, applauded by thousands of others who give "likes" and are people one may never meet. The "likes" are a momentary narcissistic reward that is not enough (and they would not be enough even if they were tens of thousands) to fill the emptiness that Juan feels. Because without spontaneous gesture, there is no bond or creation, there is no experience of being; it is not possible to say "I am," "I exist," "I choose," "I love." Juan is currently working on these issues in his psychotherapy. He decided to stop hiding behind false and meaningless profiles and to immerse himself in his self-knowledge, in search and construction of his life commitments. In this process, he understands that, for example, he values the construction of real bonds. These may complement face-to-face and virtual encounters, but they must be encounters, not monologues or expositions that one performs or observes passively.

The relationship between narcissism and the false self and social media and other socialization platforms is complex and interdependent. In short, both subjective tendencies find a convenient channel of expression in social media; at the same time, the use they make of virtuality ends up increasing them. There are certain specific personality traits (through interaction of the innate temperamental aspect and the character aspect constructed in the environmental context) that may be more or less linked to narcissism and inauthenticity. However, every person has some narcissistic and false aspects, and certain dynamics of virtual life seem to be an invitation to feed them. Ultimately, however, virtuality is nothing more than a tool or a channel, the definition of which will depend on its more or less conscientious use.

Individually, people suffering from a distress linked to narcissism and inauthenticity—such as emptiness, the feeling of not being real, of not having meaningful human bonds—may benefit from psychotherapy. We will not delve deeper into clinical work (for that, please refer to the bibliography for this section, especially Kohut, Winnicott, and Mitchell). We will only say that the therapist has to work from a position of empathic support and care, which also includes establishing the limit and the connection with reality. From that base of relational holding, this process of self-discovery, nourishment of the spontaneous gesture, and reconnection with reality will help the person to discover what values, what meaning, what way of being-in-the-world authentically appeal to them (here the therapeutic work can be guided by Frankl, May, Yalom, Schneider, Martínez Ortiz, and Martinez Robles, among others). Thus, in general terms, even outside the therapeutic space, emotional bonding and commitment to a valued meaning are ways of dealing with the aforementioned problems. Another powerful resource is creativity, which, as Winnicott (1986/2011a) said is the "doing that arises out of being" (p. 48). Since creativity is an expression of the true self, creative stimulation, in the form in which it specifically calls upon the person, will surely help to bond with and nurture one's own spontaneous gesture. The creative deployment through art, sports, work, a project, love, etc., involves at the same time a manifestation of our self, our existence, and its contribution to the world.

The virtual dimension can help to increase these existential–spiritual resources. As long as we use it as more than a showcase and for the "likes," which do no harm in moderate doses and can be part of a range of interaction factors: a video call, a heartfelt message, a virtual meeting where we are predisposed to listen and exchange. Social media and the various apps and platforms we use are contact and communication tools. By default, if we use them automatically, they may facilitate narcissistic and inauthentic problems by accentuating subjective immaturity and fragility. In this regard, they entail an alarming and regressive sociocultural phenomenon related to the addiction to success, fragmentation, narcissistic individualism, and the protagonism of the result to the detriment of the process. Their responsible, conscientious, and purposeful use, on the other hand, may involve dialoguing with a loved one who lives on the other side of the world, finding out how they are doing, telling them how you are, and many other forms of meaningful encounters with others. On a more global scale, their use may involve the multiplication of the interdependence of bonded individualities in various solidarity networks.

Over the course of the pandemic, there have been several demonstrations in this regard. In the psychological area, there were mental health organizations that provided free counseling and care to those who needed it (the School of Psychology of the University of Buenos Aires and the *Red Solidaria de Acompañamiento Psicosocial* (Solidarity Network of Psychosocial Support) in Argentina are two examples). Facebook and Instagram groups were also created where several psychologists who are mindfulness instructors have been interspersed to guide meditations periodically and free of charge, as a form of prevention and prophylaxis against the crisis (for example, the network of psychologists "*Juntos por todos*" (together for everyone). For years, solidarity organizations have learned to take advantage of the massive dissemination possibilities of social media (despite the limits of the digital divide), to summon wills and actions, as in the case of the Red Solidaria, which emerged in Argentina and has been replicated in different parts of the world.

However, it may be worthwhile to return to the world of beauty on Instagram, where Juan had lost himself like so many others, and to show, instead, the case of someone who has done something different in that very same context: hairdresser and stylist Vicky Stefani. To this day, she has thousands of followers and makes a fairly classic use of Instagram, both in relation to the promotion of her business and brands, as well as in the permanent exposure of her image. However, in the middle of the strict lockdown of 2020, she used the social network as a creative and supportive resource. As she explained, her anguish over the lack of daily work and contact with people, the economic uncertainty, and the need to contribute came together. She gave free advice on how to dye and care for hair over the course of several live videos. She went through the entire dyeing process simultaneously with her followers, whom she answered and advised on the spot without mentioning any brands. In an article in the local newspaper *La Nación* and on her Instagram, she explained that this gave her the possibility to face isolation in a different way and to make a small contribution so that people could take care of their appearance during the generalized crisis. Many people have thanked her for this gesture and the virtual space shared during the period of isolation; hundreds of them dyed their hair in sync with Vicky and received her feedback after she saw the photos of how they did it. This had a positive effect on the morale of both parties. In Vicky's case, we may infer that by providing a service based on her authentic creativity, ability, and vocation, she ended up rediscovering both herself and others. This experience was made possible by the same social network that multiplied Juan's discomfort. Hence, the constant reflection on the use of social media.

Addiction to Being Connected and Difficulty in Being Present

Paradoxically, the intensification of the virtual channel during the pandemic has facilitated both the addiction to being connected and the continuity of the encounter with the other, which is a way of healing the previous addiction. Among several variables, the excessive use of the Internet and several digital technologies is often both a cause and a consequence of relationship and emotional problems. On the other hand, the illusion created by social media of being in several places at the same time generates a vicious cycle between the widespread fear of missing out on something (FOMO), the problematic use of social media, a volatile attention, and the difficulty in being present in one's own life experiences and in relation to others. In other words, the sociocultural and individual addiction to being connected, especially linked to social media, feeds back into the fragmentation of attention on several devices and platforms at the same time, which in turn hinders the possibility of being present in one's own experiences and in relation to the other and the world. Likewise, addictions are usually related to a gap in one's own life experience; as it is not only a clinical problem but also a cultural one, we may speak of a collective existential void.

After the massive spread of computers and the Internet at the end of the last century, their problematic use began to be documented and studied. Several studies have shown symptoms equivalent to those produced by classic substance abuse addictions and other behavioral addictions such as pathological gambling: mood swings, withdrawal, tolerance, difficulty in quitting, relapse. This new addiction also been related to social anxiety, attention deficit, depression, problems in social interactions, low levels of family functioning, and life satisfaction (Cheng & Yee-Iam Li, 2014; Dresp, 2020; Hussain & Pontes, 2019). Likewise, negative changes in neuron functioning have been registered as a result of the problematic use of the Internet and technology: dysregulation in areas of the frontal cortex linked to impulse control and inhibition and in areas linked to planning and decision making; and also in the dopaminergic systems, especially the one involved in the brain reward circuit (Cerniglia et al., 2017; Dresp, 2020).

Since the rapid virtualization of all areas of life during the pandemic, the use of the Internet and its various related technologies has increased for the vast majority of people in the world. The connection of the world's population to the Internet reached 59.5% at the beginning of 2021, an increase of 7.3% over 2020, and 53% of the global population was connected to a social network, an increase of 13% (equivalent to 490 million people) over the last year (We Are Social & Hootsuite, 2021). Moreover, a Chinese study registered that over the course of the pandemic, 46% of people reported an increased dependence on Internet use, while the prevalence of severe dependence rose from 3.5% of the population to 4.3% (Sun et al., 2020).

The adolescent age group is the population at greatest risk in relation to this new form of dependence, especially linked to the excessive use of social media. The reason lies in the significance for the adolescent of the construction of identity and the emotional need to find recognition among peers and form groups of belonging in interaction with the current virtualization of life and its role in socialization. Several studies confirm the importance of family support, secure attachment patterns, and the related development of emotional regulation as protective factors with respect to excessive use of the Internet and social media (Arrivillaga et al., 2020; Blinka et al., 2020; Cerniglia et al., 2017). In other words, the relational dimension is a key factor in this contemporary problem, which is particularly widespread among the younger generations.

In general, two hypotheses have been considered regarding the main variable that determines the epidemiological risk of problematic Internet use in different societies: One is the availability of technological resources and its correlative socioeconomic level, and the other is the actual quality of life and the level of life satisfaction. An international meta-analysis (Cheng & Yee-Iam Li, 2014) registered that the higher the quality of life (measured by registering subjective perception of life satisfaction and general environmental, economic, and health data), the lower the prevalence to Internet addiction, and vice versa. However, in the study, the widespread hypothesis of availability of technological resources and high socioeconomic capacity was not found to be valid in itself. We may relate these results to the analysis of existential psychiatrist Viktor Frankl (1978/2014), who argued that the core of human well-being is a life with meaning and fulfillment, even beyond contextual conditioning factors. In other words, the contextual factor conditions variable is not a determining factor. Finding or building life purpose is a path of personal development and, at the same time, a proven protection and treatment factor in the case of various types of addiction (Martínez Ortiz et al., 2015; Martínez Ortiz, 2009).

Based on the research conducted by different authors and psychological perspectives, we may say that the lack of social-emotional bonding and the lack of meaning in life are very significant variables in the activation and maintenance of a dependency, both in terms of substance use and behaviors, including the problematic use of the Internet and social media. The other side of the coin is that both the existential faculty of finding meaning and committing to it, as well as the relational capacity to strengthen genuine human bonds (I–Thou encounter), can be nurtured as resources for prevention and treatment.

The case of Juan, presented in the previous section on narcissism and inauthenticity, once again serves as an example of how dependence on social media, meaninglessness, and a lack of attachment are intertwined. Even in his singular problem, Juan reflects how the three elements can form a vicious cycle: the emptiness and the need for recognition from others lead him to post and anxiously wait for "likes" in a powerful activation of the brain's reward circuit; but, at the same time, those "likes" are never enough and reproduce the need and anxiety to post, be connected, observe what his ideal influencers upload, and receive more and more the supposed recognition from others in a spiral that represents the aspect of tolerance that multiplies in every addiction. As Juan himself comes to understand in his personal therapy, the way in which this contact unfolds through an inauthentic and purposeless profile cannot generate real bonds, and it reproduces his emotional distress and dependence.

A more specific case of problematic internet use, intertwined with another dependency, also helps to understand the addictive dynamics that technology and the potential algorithmic confinement of contemporary virtuality may contain. It also reflects the impulsivity, momentary pleasure, and lack of control that characterize these behavioral problems of dependence, where addiction intersects with the so-called impulse control disorders (Eguiluz & Segarra, 2017; Casas et al., 2011; Alonso, 2011). Angela, a woman in her thirties who studied clothing design, consults a therapist due to an impulsive need to buy with no limits. This is linked to an addiction to being online that she is not aware of. Once again, meaning and bonds are fundamental, in addition to the aspect that we will develop later on about the capacity to be present that an addiction to being connected would impair. The pandemic surprised Angela, who had already been having doubts regarding her life plan. She had been working for some time in a clothing design and sales company as an administrative assistant. She had taken that job with the idea that one day she would be able to grow professionally in the field she had chosen to study: clothing design. However, almost ten years had passed and, according to her, the owners had not given her that possibility and would not do so in the future because they did not consider her capable. This affected her self-esteem, and her low self-esteem maintained this interpretation. However, she was reluctant to quit this job because times were too uncertain to think about changing jobs and giving up the financial security she had. During the pandemic, the company made several cutbacks due to the impact of declining revenues. They stopped paying her salary due to lack of solvency. Finally, Angela decided to quit. This decision brought some relief because of her need for a change. However, the lack of work led to a state of great anxiety. She was sinking deeper and deeper into two of her favorite pastimes: clothes shopping and scrolling through Instagram, especially through fashion and "lifestyle" influencer accounts.

Her weekly phone usage started to increase. As she was constantly looking at clothes, the algorithm sent her more and more of the same designs she liked. So she kept on buying—a lot. She had to ask for financing at the bank (the financial system facilitates and feeds impulsive consumption). The emptiness of the life project, the constant scrolling and shopping, which further complicated her finances, and her emotional state led her to disconnect from and damage her closest emotional bonds. Self-absorbed, anxious, and impulsive as she was, she stopped taking others into account because she also stopped registering herself. She borrowed money and lied about its use and repayment to her boyfriend, her mother, her friend (as is often the case with most addictions). This erosion of her bonds was affecting her more and more, as was the multiplication of debts. Although she had a desire to curb her periodic impulse buys, Instagram didn't help, reminding her of the dress and shoes from the latest collection, and, on top of that, on sale. Social media and their algorithmic systems are well designed for consumption. She was trapped in this tunnel with no apparent way out, until, with the support of her therapist, she asked her boyfriend for help.

Following Angela's own instructions, her boyfriend temporarily manages her money and gives her a daily allowance for what she needs to live on from day to day. She tore up her credit card in front of the therapist and got off Instagram and other social media for a while. These are basic guidelines for distancing oneself from the stimulus on which one depends, as in the case of an alcoholic who needs to get away from anything that may lead to alcohol consumption. However, being totally offline is not possible today; sometimes it's necessary to go online for some administrative purpose or even to read a menu at a bar.

The psychoeducational work on problematic use and addictions has been important, with the explanation of the activation of the neuropsychological circuit of reward and reinforcement. There are neuron systems linked to the release of dopamine that are activated and stimulated in a very powerful way with the consumption of substances and behavioral addictions both at the moment of the stimulus and in its anticipation; dopamine is released and generates an immediate sensation of pleasure greater than that of other situations of daily life (Alonso, 2011). With tolerance, the pleasure effect is lost, and there is a need to increase the stimulus linked to consumption or addictive behavior. The gap widens between this ever-increasing dose and the daily life not linked to the stimulus on which it depends. Basically, one loses the connection with pleasure in daily life and becomes more and more dependent on that single situation that ends up absorbing the person's life. This is often linked to the vicious cycle of anxiety. The higher the level of anxiety, the more one seeks to activate the sensation of immediate reward, and, when it is removed, anxiety will grow; this participates in the psychological dimension of abstinence.

Once Angela scrolls through influencers to calm her anxiety and to activate the pleasure (largely anticipatory) of the reward circuit, the pleasure is reproduced when she finds the shoe or T-shirt she wants to buy. The pleasurable sensation (sustained chemically by the dopamine that is released and psychologically by this conditioned learning) usually ends shortly after the purchase. The emptiness reappears, as well as the anxiety and the search for a new activation of the reward circuit. The scrolling accurately represents the voracity of the insatiable search for an ephemeral pleasure, which in a sense is never truly satisfied and only deepens the feeling of emptiness. On the other hand, technology feeds the impulsivity of staying online with different automatic activations that summon the person's addiction, such as Instagram or other social media notifications on the cell phone.

In general terms, with the particularities that each approach may have, three pillars of basic therapeutic work help to break this circuit that hides the emptiness: orientation toward something meaningful for the person; summoning and reinforcing their social bonds; and encouraging the presence of the person in those significant experiences. This changes the method of problem solving. In Angela's case, it involves ceasing to unconsciously seek refuge in Instagram and shopping because she ultimately feels worse that way, and, instead, connecting more and more consciously with what makes sense to her, such as her closest relationships (in her case meaning and the relational aspect are explicitly interwoven). Over time, she manages to be more present with others, to empathize and share deeply. She has relapses, which occur in most cases of addiction, but also because virtuality is no longer something that can be avoided; it is part of life. Therefore, her withdrawal from the addictive stimulus is more complex than with other forms of dependence.

Angela is going through this process. Shortly after starting therapy, she got a job as a wardrobe assistant for a television production company, which gave her some financial peace of mind and also produced two fundamental results: a sudden realization of her vocation and a way to sublimate her addiction to shopping and dependence on influencers. Through her creativity, she transforms into vitality that closeness with aesthetics that otherwise may involve a passive and pathological dependence. Today, since she is not permanently connected to the Internet, she is more connected to her emotions and registering (and regulating) her impulsivity, to her desires and her professional development, also to others and the support and richness involved in the encounter with others, in intimacy, dialogue, and altruism.

This case shows an individual problem in the field of clinical psychology that may well illustrate a formal definition of these new pathologies. However, beyond the current debate about the pathological definition of addiction or problematic Internet use (present in the absence of its conceptualization along with other behavioral addictions in the most representative diagnostic manuals, such as the DSM V and ICD 11, except in the case of video game use disorder), and cases of clinical severity, the pandemic context of social distancing and isolation accentuates a contemporary society and culture that adopt and disseminate an extreme and unhealthy attachment to being online. This in turn hides an existential void that extends collectively and individually, as argued by several contemporary thinkers like Byung Chul-Han (2016/2019) and Kirk Schneider (2017/2019; Segafredo, 2019).

In the last decade, Sherry Turkle, one of the world's leading psychological experts on our relationship with technology, has begun to seriously warn us about the negative results of our unlimited virtual connection, in contrast to her optimistic analysis of the advent of the Internet during the 1990s. In the quest to be online without pause, and, especially, connected to social media, we have become disconnected from ourselves and from others—that is, from our shared humanity. This idea is presented in her well-publicized essay, also turned into a Ted Talk, *Alone Together* (2017). There is a negative paradoxical effect in this constant connection: on the one hand, the permanent distraction during the face-to-face encounter with the other, which prevents genuine dialogue; on the other hand, this same permanent connection prevents the development of the ability to be with oneself in moments of solitude. It is worth noting that the ability to be alone is one of the greatest signs of subjective maturity. Both Winnicott's relational psychology (1965/2011b) and Yalom's existential psychology (1980/2015) come to this conclusion from different paths. From the development of this ability to be alone, one can build healthier bonds with others, in particular, loving bonds of care, respect, and reciprocal development that are not dependent or conflictive but rather interdependent. To this we must add that in order to develop this ability to be alone, emotional bonds that have sustained the initial experiences of the self are needed. That is to say, good (enough) emotional bonds are both cause and consequence of the ability to be alone.

The incessant connection to social media keeps us in a more or less illusory limbo of permanent social stimulation and distraction. This gives us the feeling that we are never really alone. At the same time, when spending time with someone, the engaging social connection and stimulation of social media may prevent one from bringing attention to the encounter; it's the classic image of a face-to-face gathering of people, each one immersed in their cell phones.

Turkle (2011/2017) explains that this more or less permanent distraction is corroding the precious human capacity for empathy, which, according to a study she cites in her essay, decreased among new generations of university students by 40% over the last 30 years. What she proposes is to return to conversations, to the spontaneous encounter with the other, where we don't edit what we say (or alter what the other says, seen, for example, with the recently added feature of speeding up voice messages on WhatsApp), or photoshop and filter what we show. In conversation one learns as much from the other as from oneself, and one develops the capacity for reflection and the richness of spontaneity. In this interaction to which one contributes and gives oneself at the same time, one opens oneself to the other, to oneself and to the bond. The addiction to being connected that hinders it is tantamount to hiding from one another and from ourselves, even though superficially we feel connected to everyone at the same time. In her TED Talk, Turkle describes a new way of being, where "I share, therefore I am": "We use technology to define ourselves by sharing our thoughts and feelings even as we're having them. If we don't have connection, we don't feel like ourselves. So what do we do? We connect more and more. But in the process, we set ourselves up to be isolated."

This problem becomes extremely harmful in some current early childhood situations, where the mother breastfeeds while looking at her cell phone instead of her baby, and where the babies themselves are raised with hours and hours of daily screen time (baby seats with tablet holders have even been marketed). A baby needs the gaze and the presence of the other who empathically holds them, in order to find themselves. Otherwise, a pathological false self will emerge. Therefore, it is not only the direct and excessive participation in the virtual dynamics that can facilitate inauthenticity, as we have analyzed in the previous section, so does the permanent distraction and the lack of a face-to-face and emotional encounter (skin to skin, gaze to gaze) in the mother–baby relationship.

It is worth noting that Turkle acknowledged in an interview (American Academy of Arts & Sciences, 2020) that during lockdown many people have put greater depth and engagement in virtual communications, in search of genuine human contact and expression. There have also been more calls and video calls seeking dialogue with the other, to be closer despite the social distancing. Paradoxically, she says that there has also been an explosion of contacts with chatbots, of people who have sought refuge in faking an exchange with a machine that is unaware of empathy and lacks a subjectivity that pierces the mystery of existence (the bot is predetermined and automatic). Turkle clearly explains how technology has great potential to generate spaces for listening and dialogue, with a dynamic and multidimensionality that can expand and deepen them (she gives the example of the positive feedback between group chat and the teaching of a class in virtual university education). But she also states that in recent years there has been a general choice, made by large technology companies, to go in the opposite direction, which produces the greatest profits for them. However, it raises a hope, which we share, that the pandemic isolation and social distancing may have catalyzed in many people the revaluation of the human encounter: registering the need to embrace one's loved ones, the return to the real bond. It may also be channeled virtually when technology is the means to that human end. Although it should be added that there are certain possibilities of the face-to-face encounter that are irreplaceable; the hug is the clearest example, as well as children's need for corporal emotional support.

The different ways of experiencing virtuality can be exemplified through the gaming modalities that have been accentuated during the pandemic. In a talk about gaming and technology during lockdown, broadcast by Instagram in mid-2020, child and adolescent psychologist Maritchu Seitun (2020) explained in dialogue with children's literature author Sofía Chas that role playing and bonded interaction games (face-to-face or virtual) reduce stress, while online games where you compete with the machine or with others objectified as enemies increase stress. The latter type of gaming not only increases stress but is iconic of addiction to being connected. This even has a neuroscientific explanation: Just as the first type of game generates hormones such as oxytocin that produce a feeling of pleasure and satiety, in the second type there is a constant production of dopamine, which generates an immediate reward and satisfaction, none of which is ever fully satiated and leads the person to seek reward and satisfaction again and again. There are kids who have peed themselves from not moving away from the computer.

The addiction to being connected makes us machine like. It distances us from our bodies and emotions, from bonds, and from our genuine life purposes. In short, it distances us from our own experience. It has to do with the inability to be present in the encounter with oneself and with the other. From the need to be online on multiple platforms and devices at the same time, we become distracted and fragment our attention automatically to the point of losing the ability to focus and be present. Research shows how the simultaneous, intense, and unaware use of multiple technological media leads to lower attention skills and increases the tendency to distraction, among other cognitive dysfunctions (Gorman & Green, 2016; Lottridge et al., 2015; van der Schuur et al., 2020).

At the same time, it is also interesting to know that multitasking is still a skill of an extremely evolved brain. In this sense, it has also been proven that if we learn to be aware, to make choices, and plan our purpose when faced with an enormous amount of stimuli, the multitasking that we have developed and the possibilities offered by different technological media may enhance our ways of knowing in the integration of different contents and the horizon of a more global vision (Lottridge et al., 2015).

However, the fragmented attention due to the uncontrolled use of multiple media, devices, and technological platforms sustains the addiction to being online. The countless ways in which digital technologies attract our attention, such as real-time alerts on our cell phones about what is happening on social media, reinforce this vicious cycle. The multiplication of FOMO, or fear of missing out, also plays a part in this. The more FOMO, the greater the need to be connected to social media in the search not to miss anything (Torres-Serrano, 2020), and the more connected, the greater the voracity of the fear of missing out. In other words, FOMO and the excessive use of the Internet feed on each other and generate different forms of emotional discomfort (F. Gil et al., 2015). There are always new stories and posts to see, profiles to check out, "fun facts" to Google, and shows to binge. The Internet is infinite. Depending on how we use it, it can be a resource of enormous wealth or a black hole that sucks us in, increasing anxiety, the need for immediate reward, insomnia, and the feeling of emptiness.

We are facing a growing trend of constant review of online experiences. If we're honest with ourselves, some of these scenes will sound familiar: chatting on WhatsApp with several friends at the same time while talking in person with another friend; being suspended on Instagram watching stories and photos of others in fantastic landscapes while in a park surrounded by trees, or perhaps watching how others react to our own photo of our landscape while we are in it (without actually being in it); swiping left or right on Tinder while having a drink at a party; and the last straw of watching a show on Netflix where the family is having dinner while having dinner with our family. We could go on with countless examples. The question that arises is very simple: If we are constantly reviewing dozens of experiences online or recording and promoting our own experiences, how do we go about being present in what we are experiencing?

The answer is that we are not present. And if we are not present in our experience, there is no way to connect with the other or to discover what we value and what makes sense to us. Presence, meaningful bonds, and meaning are intertwined in the human, individual, and collective opportunity to unravel and transform the addictive relationship with the virtual world, in a process of empowerment and awareness.

Mindfulness training can help, both through the formal practice of different meditation modalities, as well as through the informal practice of focusing on what we do on a daily basis. These practices develop a general and concrete habit of full presence in daily life (Kabat-Zinn, 1990/2016). Specifically, mindfulness has proven to be an effective technique to counteract the attention problems generated by intense and uncontrolled multitasking of technological media (Gorman & Green, 2016); it also contributes to the reduction of depressive and anxious emotional distress (Segal et al., 2013/2015; Zeidan et al., 2014). Therefore, the practice of mindfulness is an important resource for the prevention and treatment of these contemporary problems. And this philosophy, which nurtures the Being mode to balance the ruminative hypertrophy of the Doing mode, becomes almost a basic necessity of our hectic, distracted, and all-consuming contemporary way of life.

Focusing the fullest possible attention on a conversation (or some other activity of human bonding encounter) in self-reflection on that which appeals to us or simply in one's own present experience today involves constant gymnastics of the will and the mind, although originally natural. The satisfaction in this case is not immediate and all-consuming as with the dizzying and addictive dynamics of social media (or stressful online games) but involves a much longer process. As this process goes on, satisfaction will not be ephemeral, monothematic, and insatiable (as in the case of addiction) but will come to stay for a while and expand different planes of one's life.

It is not an easy feat in the context of a culture addicted to being online, which in turn is the cause and consequence of a technological business structure that is based on reproducing it. *The Social Dilemma* (Netflix documentary) clearly describes how major social media and content and digital entertainment platforms are dedicated to developing strategies to keep and attract people's attention. And so the dissemination of this documentary shows that criticism and awareness can emerge right there in the digital mainstream (the counterbalance is still negligible). The main objective of these businesses is to distract people from their daily lives in order to entice them to reconnect, in a dangerous form of attention hacking. This constant tugging makes us lose concentration, deregulates us, and makes us impulsive and passive at the same time because we have less and less control over the impulse to log in and log back in (fueled by constant warnings that "you're missing out on something"). While this dynamic activates and inflates FOMO, it can put a dent in our capacity for control, planning, and accountability.

It is necessary to protect and empower oneself in the face of this economic and cultural structure and to contribute to other possible collective frameworks that include virtuality in a different way. Together with bonds and meaning, the training of being present in one's own experience is one of the possible keys for doing so. During an Instagram Live video on mindfulness and technology with Marian Durao (2021), Martin Reynoso discussed the possibility of registering our own body, emotions, and cognitive functions to measure one's threshold for technology use. He also considered the importance of everyone being able to allow themselves moments of rest and technological cleansing, where they voluntarily put aside their cell phones and other devices for a specific period of time. On the other hand, he considered that technological multitasking is sometimes necessary, especially in specific work environments. The challenge is to develop a form of global mindfulness, which is aware of the constant change in the focus of attention and its relative simultaneous division into a multiplicity of elements, and which allows discerning when it is necessary and when it is not. This global mindfulness would integrate focused attention with an open receptivity to other stimuli in the awareness and possibility of change from the focal to the multiple. The means of dissemination of Reynoso's dialogue was the same social network on which Angela became dependent: Social networks channel what we deposit in them.

From a dimensional point of view, what in a pathological extreme manifests itself in the addiction to be constantly online and on several devices and platforms at the same time may also have a balanced, conscientious, and responsible nuance that enhances our capacity for integrative global presence. It may be a contribution to humanism and current complex thinking in circumstances of profound uncertainty. In fact, Reynoso himself clarified in that dialogue how significant the virtual space has been during the pandemic for people to initiate or maintain their mindfulness training within the framework of group meditation spaces.

What is fundamental is the chosen goal of developing our humanity. Technology as a means and channel toward that horizon is very different from technology as an end or, to return to the central theme of the section, to being connected online as an end in itself. What is the purpose of being connected or disconnected to the Internet at any given moment? If we respond with the realization of a valued meaning, there is no doubt of its benefit. It is a matter of integrating the face to face and the virtual in one's own experience with meaning, presence, and bonding.

We need to give technology its proper place—neither despise it nor idealize it. In the context of the addictive tendency to be online, there is also a disproportionate focus on technology itself as a problem solver, beyond the fact that in some cases it really is a means to solve problems. The world of apps, which is indisputably useful in various circumstances (such as paperwork, bank transactions, product purchases, etc.) has reached the point where we look there for guidance for almost everything: playing, training, taking care of our mental health, even praying. In the preface to the latest edition of *Alone Together*, Turkle (2011/2017) recounts that the first reaction of the researcher who witnessed the decline of empathy among young people was to think of creating an app for empathy. But the important thing is to understand, she says, that "we are the app for empathy." Technology and its machines, however complex they become, are existentially and relationally empty. Humanity lies in each one of us, in our freedom, our decisions, our presence, our bonds and encounters, in our history made up of joys and sorrows. The virtual world could be just another plane of our overall human experience, a medium and channel, along with others. But when it becomes an end, as in the cases of Angela and Juan, we become machines in the emptying of our experience.

Being shipwrecked in the middle of the Internet ocean requires the rehumanization brought by bonds, meaning, and presence, like the arrival of a manned ship where one takes the helm toward one's own land.

Cyberbullying, Objectification, and Social Anxiety

In the juxtaposition of the pandemic and the virtualization of life, the bond with the other has changed (and will continue to change) for better and for worse. Lockdowns and social distancing have converged to curb the spread of COVID-19 and transfer a great deal of our lives to the virtual technological world. In their problematic version, both phenomena could weaken the human encounter, and, therefore, the possibility of empathy, and facilitate a growing distance from the other and their subjectivity, which also involves a distance from one's own. The extremes are reflected in social isolation as an avoidance of bonding (beyond the need to stay safe) and in cyberbullying, which is particularly widespread among adolescents and young adults (although it is also present among adults of different ages). This distance from the other—due to its threat, its violence, and its objectification—is a major source of distress for contemporary human beings.

Several specialized researchers warn of an increase in social anxiety and the hikikomori syndrome of extreme self-isolation among the world's population as a consequence of the pandemic and social distancing (Thomson et al., 2021; Rooksby et al., 2020). The seriousness of this problem lies in its basic invisibility, accentuated by the formal framework of lockdowns and the social distancing decreed by the global health emergency. When isolating oneself is the norm, the person already suffering from social phobia can thus justify the avoidance of confronting the bond (both feared and desired), which in turn perpetuates and increases the problem. At the same time, others who have an undeclared pre-pandemic tendency toward social anxiety may find the manifestation of that difficulty in the decline of their face-to-face interaction and bonding.

On the other hand, some studies and analyses register an increase in the levels of risk and vulnerability to cyberbullying since the beginning of the pandemic (Jain et al., 2020; Agus et al., 2021). This virtual form of harassment, which had been on the rise in recent years prior to COVID-19, particularly affects the adolescent and young adult population but does not exclude children or middle-aged adults. Cyberbullying involves the use of virtuality and various technological devices to perform acts intended to hurt or embarrass another person (Chakraborty et al., 2021). It differs from classic harassment in that the victimizer may remain anonymous (which is half the time), and the content used to mistreat the victim reaches a wider audience and may remain online indefinitely. Likewise, the disinhibitory effect of virtuality facilitates the aggressiveness toward others displayed by bullies. Technology allows abuse to be present around the clock, in complete anonymity, and often without consequences. The likelihood of a cybervictim suffering from a mental health problem is double that of a traditional victim of bullying. In other words, virtuality aggravates the imbalance of power between victim and victimizer in several ways (Ansary, 2020; Chakraborty et al., 2021).

A situation that became public during the pandemic, experienced by Argentine music journalist Bebe Contepomi, reflects the indefinite multiplication of harassment facilitated by social media. The journalist recounted the explosive viralization of fragments of an interview conducted through his Instagram, where some of his gestures were interpreted as signs of drug use by different users who mocked him, many of them protected by anonymity. The taunts multiplied on Twitter and other social networks to the point that for a few days he answered several calls from family and friends asking him if he was okay. A week later, Contepomi had a car crash, which he attributed to the emotional distress generated by the cyberbullying. "It was just a 10-second video, where you could see a tic of mine, but at one point it was all too overwhelming. Everything they say about you is so harsh that you start second-guessing yourself, and you wonder if you need to go out and apologize. It was nonstop for three days," said the journalist, in an article published in Argentine newspaper *La Nación* on May 24, 2020. Beyond the fact that Contepomi is a public figure (this involves certain particularities, which we will not get into here), this experience shows the multiplying effect of cyberbullying, as well as its negative effect on the self-esteem and emotional state of the person who suffers it and who may even start thinking they really did something wrong; this happens at any age.

Specifically among children and adolescents, the main problems related to cyberbullying are excessive Internet consumption or addiction to being connected, lack of parental supervision and support (Romera et al., 2021; Feijóo et al., 2021), low self-esteem (Brewer & Kerslake, 2015) among both victims and victimizers (Ansay, 2020), lack of empathy among victimizers (Brewer & Kerslake, 2015), and social anxiety among victims (Ruíz-Martín et al., 2019).

An important issue to highlight is that cybervictims and cyberbullies have much in common, both in terms of risk factors and the negative psychosocial consequences of cyberbullying, which include different forms of emotional distress. In fact, there is a percentage of those involved in this problem that from time to time switch between the roles of victim and victimizer. For example, according to recent studies, of the 14% of Spanish children and adolescents involved in cyberbullying, 5.2% are victims, 4.5% are victimizers, and 4.3% are both at the same time (Feijóo et al., 2021). In both roles of this problem, there are multiple bonding failures in the primary family environment, at school, and with peers in general. Likewise, among the main protective factors are good bonds between child and father or mother, peer interaction and support, as well as a positive school climate. These are also related to the other protective factors considered to be intrapersonal, such as good self-esteem, social skills, and emotional management (Ansary, 2020).

There are several specific and meta-analytical studies (such as those cited above) that demonstrate what has been said so far with respect to victims and victimizers. Less is said about and focused on the countless witnesses of this mistreatment of the other in the shared virtual space. A European Union report on various forms of cyberhate states that 80% of adolescents reportedly witnessed cyberbullying and that the vast majority of them did not intervene in the situation. One of the explanations is that virtual anonymity and mediatization deepen the distance not only between victim and victimizer but also between observer and victim (Rudnicki & Steiger, 2020). The "other" would thus be just another user among the millions online, without a particular subjectivity (a history, longings, and feelings) with which the observer empathizes. The gravity and power of cyberbullying lies in the multiplied dissemination of abuse that extends far beyond the moment of the aggression itself as in traditional bullying. The tens, hundreds, thousands, millions of witnesses of that harassment, most of whom remain (as do we) passive, allow this multiplication of mistreatment with its silent connection. From a global perspective, narcissism (Han, 2016/2019), robotic mode (Schneider, 2017/2019), and the decline of empathy (Turkle, 2011/2017), which in general promote the dynamics of the virtual world, provide important variables to understand this phenomenon.

The instrumentalization and objectification of the other is facilitated by anonymity and the increasingly accentuated mediatization among people. When we say progressive mediatization, we refer to a communication that gradually erases the personal characteristics of the other, or the characteristics of the encounter itself, as a dialogical I–Thou exchange. For example, a synchronous video call, although clearly mediated communication, is less mediated than a voice message to a contact in the social network itself, which in turn is less mediated than a text message in a virtual forum with strangers using a nickname. This doesn't mean that an extremely mediatized communication such as the latter cannot consider the other person in order to generate a genuine human encounter. It simply means greater distance and difficulty in doing so.

When mediatization involves anonymity, disinhibition is accentuated and a kind of potential dissociation that is typical in virtual interactions deepens. In turn, the lack of presence and, therefore, of physical proximity, blurs the responsibility to the limit of performing acts that one would not do in person, even more so when they are hidden by the veil of anonymity (Chakraborty et al., 2021). Self-awareness and personal ethics change, together with the distancing from the other and from one's own capacity for empathy.

As we have argued from the beginning, the problem is not technological mediatization per se but its uncritical and humanly irresponsible use. Disregarding the other as a free, unique, multidimensional being, in becoming and, in one way or another, linked to oneself (even if it is in the sharing of the human condition), involves this irresponsible use, which translates into the objectification of the other. We return again to the central dilemma: In this inevitable and dizzying virtualization of life, do we become mechanized and dehumanized, or do we channel humanity through technology?

In an interview published by the journal of the Latin American Association of Existential Psychotherapy (Segafredo, 2021), psychologist Ramiro Gómez Salas states that technological instrumentalization has shaped a problematic way of being, with a significant lack of relationships and encounters:

> The inability of contemporary man to donate himself makes his existence like that of an internaut: he skirts along the surface of immense knowledge and experiences, but he is not able to immerse himself. There is a depth to discover in the other, a deep subjectivity beneath the surface of their skin. Insofar as you don't have that depth, you can be subject to exploitation, to use. The moment I discover that behind your gaze there is a content, a story, someone like me, but different from me... the utilitarian search for people ends. (p. 40)

In cyberbullying, victimizers and indifferent observers ignore the subjective depth of the victim. The other becomes a thing on which one can unload as much violence, fear, and frustration as one wants, without apparent consequences, but also a thing through which the apathy of the cyberwitness is very easily displayed. Technological mediatization, as we have said, can facilitate this problem. How many times have we come across a video forwarded in a WhatsApp group or reposted on a social network, where there is real mistreatment and humiliation of the other, however subtle it may be? How do we respond to this? Watching it on WhatsApp is not the same as witnessing it live, where the victim's emotional response after the fact is not edited out, where one cannot simply close the video and in a second go from connection to disconnection with the other and what is happening.

The case of Federico, a 9-year-old boy, illustrates this situation in everyday life, in which children and adults can participate through action or omission. Federico is the youngest of three children in the context of a conflictive parental separation. At one point in the pandemic, he no longer wants to enter classes through Zoom and becomes very nervous at the prospect of doing so; some of his classmates tease him with anonymously created stickers and backgrounds alluding to his weight, which have been spread through Zoom and the WhatsApp group. Prior to this, some of his classmates had begun to disconnect him from virtual games as a way of mocking him. This made him increasingly angry and inhibited him. Those who initiate the taunts are few, but all the rest watch without saying anything. Here adults are also involved: When Federico's mother contacts other mothers in the class and in a virtual meeting tries to find empathy and the possibility of an agreement, she is met with minimization of the fact and even anger at the "accusation."

We cannot know whether a hypothetical face-to-face witnessing of these exchanges would have changed the situation and awareness of the bullying. However, we do know that Federico's distress, after being disconnected from the games or seeing the stickers, did not appear on screen; he was "out of frame." And that the objectification and violence suffered are perpetuated in the production and reproduction of the sticker. A sticker is a cut-out and generally expressive image that can be sent from contact to contact in an unlimited number of ways. Thus, perhaps Federico's image, which contains a mockery of his body and assaults his subjectivity, may be resending itself at this moment over and over again. The person who receives it does not know the anguish that Federico experienced, how it hurt his self-image and how it affected his interpretation of being worthy of affection from others to the point of feeling undeserving of friendships; nor do they know how it accentuated a latent emotional instability due to his parents' conflictive separation. This subjective and human depth, with which we can come into contact through empathy, disappears in the flatness of the sticker, which is the only thing that remains, as if it were a digital doll.

Those who study the tremendous dissemination throughout the virtual sphere of hate speeches (where violent political and social positions of exclusion, xenophobia, and racism are manifested) also recognize in mediatization a space that facilitates the distance from the other and their objectification as an object of hate, as opposed to the human faculty of empathizing with others (Rudnicki & Steiger, 2020). Kirk Schneider (Segafredo, 2019) associates this rising paradigm, which is also manifested in the growth of followers and voters of extremist parties in several world democracies, with the idea of a "polarized mind," which fails to integrate what's different both within oneself and the other, and to which, consequently, one responds with rejection and fear. On the other hand, the "paradoxical self" that manages to understand the other, to bond with them, also involves being present with the other (and one's own other) in oneself. To encounter the other is to encounter oneself, and the violence projected onto the other is rooted in what we reject or are afraid of in ourselves. Indifference is an accomplice to the advancement of that polarized mind. Likewise, the tendencies of distress described in the previous sections participate in the vicious cycle of this problem: narcissism and inauthenticity, addiction to being connected, and the difficulty of being present—which involve a disconnection with diversity, with what is genuine, and with what characterizes us existentially as humans.

The focus of any intervention to address cyberbullying (and the social trend it represents) among victimizers, victims, and witnesses will be on deepening the bond with the other, sharing one's own experience, nurturing empathy, listening, encountering in its richness as an unfolding of our relational existence. In cognitive terms, it refers to cultivating social and emotional skills (Agus et al., 2021). This goes hand in hand with leaving one's own narcissism and the state of being "connected" but absent. Let's also remember the appeal made by contemporary philosopher Byung-Chul Han (2016/2019) to recover the capacity for listening and community. This search needs to be implemented both individually and collectively, in the integration of the virtual and the face to face.

An approach to this problem that does not include the virtual space would be a failure, at least in the medium and long term. Psychoeducation and possible social responses disseminated online through prevention campaigns and direct intervention in situations of cyberbullying (e.g., through rules of coexistence on social media) are the obvious collective benefit of addressing the issue, including virtuality. The possibility of reporting cyberbullying through the virtual world, as well as the existence of forums where bad experiences can be shared, have proven to be very good resources for intervention. (Chakraborty et al., 2021). Even from the clinical point of view, activating conscious responses and actions in the virtual context entails a contemporary benefit and demand. The issue will be to change the spaces and forms of bonding in digital interaction when someone suffers from cyberbullying (regardless of their role in the scene). At the same time (and this is fundamental), we mustn't forget that the "we are the app for empathy" (Turkle, 2011/2017) and that to "upload" and "update" it what we need is to meet and have spontaneous face-to-face conversations with others without the flattening of filters, photoshopping, and editing. Therefore, it is essential to include face-to-face exchange with others in any intervention proposal, as well as in health prevention and promotion. In other words, in the best-case scenario, the perspective will be hybrid: face to face and virtual.

Another generality, both for the clinic and for prevention, is to nurture the meaning that the human encounter itself can have and, particularly, the encounters where the person (or the group of people) share some meaning with the other. We should aim at self-transcendence (Frankl, 1946/2013) and creativity itself (Winnicott, 1965/2011b; Fromm, 1947/2007a) in relation to another person or the world at large. That is to say, to get out of one's own self-absorption (whether as a victim, victimizer, or observer) and move toward what we genuinely feel is worthwhile, thus contributing something to the world through our subjective transformation of reality and even anguish. Two activities that explicitly alchemize it are art and sports, although they are not the only ones.

The story of Jennifer Dahlgren, an Argentine Olympic athlete, writer, and a leader in raising awareness of bullying and cyberbullying, is revealing. Jenny, as she likes to be called, suffered traditional bullying as a child for having a different body type than her schoolmates. Both in her 2016 TED Talk *El martillo volador* (The flying hammer) and in her eponymous book of children's stories, she recounts the deep emotional suffering and wounds to her self-esteem that she experienced as a result of abuse and discrimination during her adolescence. She also recounts the importance of sports, and nowadays, writing, when it comes to healing those wounds. In sports, she found new ways to encounter others from a shared meaning, from the effort and sacrifice for shared values and goals, which was a way to encounter herself. In athletics, specifically in the hammer throw, she developed self-transcendence and a powerful transformative creativity, where the body that had been teased for being taller and bigger than others became a strength. As she says in one of her stories, through sports she transformed the difference for which she was discriminated against into an extraordinary virtue. Finding this meaning not only led to several sporting achievements but also helped her to accept and appreciate herself as she is. Likewise, after winning three South American championships, a bronze medal in the Pan American Games, and participating four times in the Olympics, Jenny captured her story through writing, which also functioned as a way to alchemize her previous suffering into vitality and wealth for others. Through her stories, she raises awareness of bullying and also of the ways of healing through the creative living of the body in sports (and, indirectly, through art as well).

Another interesting aspect of the case is that Jenny reflects on the possibility of turning the virtual space (both social media and other digital media) into a channel for awareness and healing. Jenny represents the counterpart to the current trend of bringing bullying into the digital realm and also to the trend toward a homogenizing and inauthentic social media aesthetic. By the latter, we mean the photoshopping, filtering, and critiquing of different bodies. Although in this work we touch peripherally on this issue that conditions body self-image and self-esteem (the problem lies, among other variables, in the global cultural objectification of bodies, especially female bodies), it is related to the landscape described in the section on narcissism and inauthenticity. We may briefly say that there is an aesthetic trend, propitiated by the dynamics of social media like Instagram and its most successful influencers' profiles, of erasing imperfections and Barbiefication of bodies. Taken to everyday life, this digital editing of the body and the elimination of its own features in the copy of virtual kings and queens, may be understood as a veiled sociocultural cyberbullying and self-cyberbullying (by photoshopping ourselves). Not to mention the explicit criticism of the body of the other, so recurrent in cyberbullying itself.

By contrast, Jenny Dahlgren shows the capacity for multiplication and dissemination of virtuality in relation to respect for the emotions and the body of the other, to consider the validity and richness of what's different. She is part of massive social prevention campaigns collaborating with agencies like UNICEF and Argentina's INADI; she also performs small daily acts of awareness through her posts on her Instagram and Facebook accounts, with reflections and depictions of her daily life. She is thus genuinely committed to this mission from her history and from her own body. There is a clear meaning in her use of social media, which demonstrates this other possibility that is latent in them, the deployment of which depends on who and how they use them.

Although the majority of the population involved in cyberbullying is comprised of cyberwitnesses (and this is where social interventions could be focused), therapists are most likely to receive consultations from cybervictims. These fulfill the role of one who is humiliated by another and marginalized either from a particular group, or, simply, from the group that is not mistreated. The cybervictim shares the aspect of marginalization and the problematic relational experience with those who suffer from social anxiety. In fact, the latter is a risk factor for cyberbullying (Ruíz-Martin et al., 2019). That is, fearing others and their negative assessment may predispose one to being rejected by them, in a kind of self-fulfilling prophecy.

On the cognitive–behavioral level, which helps explain certain generalities of mental experience, social anxiety involves constantly interpreting that the other will judge us negatively, and also engaging in repetitive behavior that avoids that contact. Fernández-Álvarez and Bogiazian (2008), present a clear definition: "It is a form of fear before the direct or indirect observation of others, which involves a set of emotional, visceral, and postural reactions associated with representations of the individual that refer to alleged negative judgments of others regarding their behavior or their personal qualities" (p. 29). There are varying degrees of severity, ranging from social anxiety in specific situations such as public speaking (classified as discreet) to generalized social anxiety that involves distress in most social situations. The extreme case may reach total isolation that makes it impossible for the person to have satisfactory interactions with others and a satisfactory work and emotional life (based on the subjective interpretation itself rather than on standards). Fernández-Álvarez and Bogiazian (2008) explain that the main desire of those who have social anxiety, "the invisible man," is to be able to be in the situations that interest them, among others, but without being detected by them. But are you present in a situation if you do not share it in some way with others? There is an interesting film that from another place seeks to answer this same question. *Into the Wild* tells the story of a young man who, due to philosophical convictions, decides to isolate himself from contemporary society and go into the wilderness of Alaska, where he undergoes profound experiences that he writes about in a diary, until he realizes that for these to really have meaning, he needs to share them with others. Can there be experience and being with no relationships?

Returning to the supposed desire to be invisible, the pandemic has granted this wish for some in part by mediating and giving anonymity to so many encounters (having the camera off at a Zoom meeting is also a way of making one's presence more anonymous and of avoiding the other's gaze). The risk of contagion also accentuated the perception of threat in the contact with the other; although viral transmission and potential rejection of the person are different forms of threat, the encounter with the other becomes doubly "risky." On a deeper level, realizing that desire to be invisible could also mean not being oneself. We should clarify that there are fundamental differences between the introverted personality, whose primary trait is shyness, and the person with social phobia, whose main feeling usually involves embarrassment (Fernández-Álvarez & Bogiazian, 2008). This embarrassment is felt at the moment something is done and especially in anticipation of what the person might do or show in front of the other (including anxious reactions such as sweating or blushing generated by those same thoughts).

When we say that being invisible could mean not being oneself, we refer to the existential and emotional fact that the avoidance of the other impoverishes the life experience not only on an evident plane of labor and social functionality but also in the global reality of the bio-psychosocial-spiritual self, which does not develop if there is no significant bonding (manifested or internalized). If I cannot be who I am in front of others, when I am alone do I know who I am?

We have already discussed the fundamental role of bonding for the development (survival, deployment, and well-being) of the person's subjectivity. We may sum up that for the human being the emotional bonding relationship is fundamental in the beginning; this is literally so in the newborn and is the structural basis of the construction that involves the self in the adult. From the relational perspective, it is proposed that the person develops the capacity to be alone only when they have reached a certain psychological and emotional maturity (Winnicott, 1965/2011b) because they will have internalized a good enough emotional bond that has empathically recognized their spontaneous gesture, and, thus, has facilitated the construction of their true self. This bonding pattern, which determines the type of attachment (secure or insecure) and is an important variable in our capacity to explore the world, has its origin in primary relationships but is updated and energized in significant interactions throughout life (Bowlby, 1969/2012; Marrone, 2009). Failures in primary supportive and attachment bonds may be an important dimension in the configuration of social anxiety, among other mental health problems; they often involve a negative view of the self, the other, or both. Research has shown a direct correlation between insecure attachment (especially anxious and ambivalent or preoccupied attachment) and high levels of social anxiety, and between secure attachment and subjective well-being (Conrad et al., 2021; Öztürk & Mutlu, 2010).

In children and adolescents, the pandemic and its social distancing seem to have deepened the significance of primary bonds in their representation of themselves, others, and the world because, for example, with virtual schooling and periods of lockdown, the possibilities of finding emotional support and some form of relational base in alternative figures, such as teachers or other family members outside of the home, have been limited. In the case of adolescents, a major limitation of the natural process of coming out into the world is added. Therefore, the distance of a possible satisfactory encounter with the other becomes bigger and more difficult. Social anxiety symptoms find a breeding ground here.

Cecilia is 14 years old, the daughter of a single mother; she has an older sister who lives in another city and with whom she has little contact. Before the pandemic, even though she was a shy and somewhat insecure girl, she had friendships with schoolmates, nurtured by gatherings within the school environment and a few sporadic invitations to the homes of two friends. During the first lockdown in Argentina, which lasted about eight months, contact with those friends moved to the virtual realm through social media like TikTok and Instagram (where she hardly uploads photos and stories, and mainly observes those uploaded by others), and video games like Minecraft; but this contact was lost little by little, until they stopped talking altogether. Cecilia stayed at home with her mother, who for various reasons (a traumatic childhood and recent relationship history, among others) has not been able to support Cecilia emotionally as she would have needed and has always presented characteristics of an unstable and ambivalent attachment figure.

With the return to face-to-face classes at the beginning of 2021, Cecilia returned to school and, even with difficulties and a certain nervousness before approaching them, she gradually got back in touch with her friends. Again they began to cross paths and to talk to one another at recess. They spontaneously organized a few outings after school. Her mood improved greatly in those weeks. But then schools closed again, Cecilia lost contact with her friends, and her spirits fell. Soon after, she passed one of her two friends on the street; out of anxiety over meeting them, she waved at them, pretended to be in a hurry, and kept on walking. She later regretted that and was sad that she had not stopped to talk to them. She finds herself in this situation when in the therapeutic space she expresses her need to find a way to communicate with her friends and, in the best-case scenario, to meet face to face. The proposed idea of contacting them directly by

WhatsApp seems impractical to her. She interprets that her friends are not interested in talking to her because they have not sent her messages recently. For that reason she says she could not text them either. The fear of being rejected has been strongly installed in the context of social distancing. However, she agrees to subtly react to some Instagram stories posted by her friends if the opportunity arises, and thus reactivate an exchange with the aim of organizing a gathering, whether or not classes return. In other words, virtuality could function as a momentary intermediate space to help her reconnect with her friends.

Cecilia does not present symptoms of what some call clinical social anxiety but rather subclinical signs or simply a tendency, socially significant because it is to be expected in introverted and shy adolescents during lockdown, even more so in the case of having attachment figures that do not generate security. That said, the first thing Cecilia's case teaches us is the importance of the school as a socialization environment and as a transitional space for the adolescent's exogamous process in pursuit of individuation and autonomy. On the other hand, just as we have talked about the relationship problems that technological mediatization can facilitate, Cecilia's case shows that the virtual space can also be a bridge for people with relationship difficulties and inhibitions. The technologically mediated situation can help to make the encounter with the other not so "compromising" and massive. We have also analyzed this with respect to sexual–emotional relationships and dating apps in the previous chapter. In any case, in Cecilia's situation, the repeated face-to-face encounters at school have allowed the bond blockage to dissolve; however, the sudden face-to-face chance encounter in the street after weeks of isolation and distance proved to be excessive at the time.

Alberto, on the other hand, is almost 60 years old and is a very reserved man who experiences significant anxiety in social situations. The case and its issues predate the pandemic. Until discovering social media and since his youth, Alberto's interactions were limited to a very closed circle of loved ones. But through the internet, he started to get in touch and interact with several acquaintances through posts, comments, and messages. His social life took on a new dimension. However, Alberto was not able to take the step toward arranging face-to-face encounters. Using Winnicott's (1971/2015) conceptualizations with some leeway, we may think of virtuality as a transitional space between being bodily present with the other and not being so. This bridging "place" seems to have an enormous value in these cases where there are internal and relational reasons (bearing in mind that nothing is purely internal and nothing is purely relational, but both at the same time) that hinder the spontaneous encounter with the other in daily life. Even when there are external reasons that prevent a face-to-face meeting, such as a pandemic, virtuality is established as an intermediate space between being able to see and embrace a loved one and not being able to do so. At the same time, as in Alberto's case, there is a risk of getting stuck in the intermediate place and of not completing the step to reach the genuine and imperfect present body encounter.

In order to complement the importance of bonding in these issues, it might be of interest to take up the existential perspective that considers that one of the fundamental human problems is to accept that there is a plane in which each one of us is alone (Yalom, 1980/2015). There are intimate experiences that each person lives in solitude even if they share them with others, and they may be accompanied in that. In fact, in order to be able to bond emotionally with another person without dependence or selfishness, it is necessary to accept this experience of one's own solitude. Erich Fromm (2007b) integrates that existential perspective with the relational one, explaining that during the individuation process the person becomes increasingly autonomous and separated from others (in the first place, from parents), until they become independent. It is only at that moment that they can encounter the other and deploy their creativity through genuine love that does not fuse (or disdain, as an antithesis) but bonds these two autonomous persons in subjective interdependence. On the other hand, Martin Buber (1923/2013) proposes a relational existential view, where the I–Thou unveils and develops who we are. It not only refers to the interaction with the other but to opening oneself up to an intimate bond in which I am with the other, in which we are and are becoming in this dialogue—a bond that deepens our experience of being.

In both social anxiety and cyberbullying, there is a discomfort closely related to past and present bonding deficiencies, which have repercussions on the self and its capacity for solitude, autonomy, and, therefore, current relationships. In the case of cyberbullying, there is a harm to the other that is done, observed, or suffered, and even the victimizer and the observer end up suffering it as well. Because by objectifying the Thou, the I loses the I–Thou interaction that humanizes it. In the case of social anxiety, isolation and avoidance of the other degrade the life experience and corrode the self, which does not unfold without bonding (explicit or internalized). There's reliance on a relationship that does not come to fruition (in some cases because it was not there in the first place). In both forms of distress, there is an impoverishment of the experience of being, and, thus, an open trench through which the feeling of emptiness and emotional suffering can run.

Regarding interventions to address the tendency toward social anxiety, we will take up some of the issues already mentioned with regard to cyberbullying and add others. Our perspective proposes relational and existential guidelines to be integrated into prevention and health promotion projects, as well as individual and group treatments. We also consider that in clinical cases of severe social anxiety, our proposal should be complemented with cognitive–behavioral approaches (sometimes it may even be necessary to add psychopharmacological treatment), which refer to social skills training, exposure techniques, systematic desensitization, and cognitive restructuring (Vallejo-Slocker & Vallejo, 2016; Vallejo Ruiloba, 2011; Bados López & García Grau, 2011; Fernández-Álvarez & Bogiaizian, 2008; Baeza Velazco, 2007); these can be studied in depth through the bibliography cited above. In the psychotherapeutic practice with these cases, it will also be advisable to apply the clinical treatment that arises from attachment theory, with respect to providing a secure base in the therapeutic relationship through empathic sensitivity, regular availability, and emotional and assertive communication (Marrone, 2009). The change in intersubjectivity and in the exploration of the world that this involves (as well as of one's own vision of oneself) may thus begin in the experience of the bond with the therapist.

Similar to the general ways in which to deal with cyberbullying, nurturing the meaning of human encounters, and, more than anything else, meaningful encounters for the people who participate in them, make it possible to revitalize wounded relational existence. Cecilia, for example, during treatment rediscovered a latent bond with a cousin her same age, who likes to do gymnastics and yoga like her. Cecilia was already looking forward to starting some form of physical activity. She resumed contact with her cousin, and they arranged to go twice a week to a nearby park. The interaction itself, and the idea of the sharing gymnastics, revitalized Cecilia and gave her considerable relief from her isolation.

The unfolding of the person's creativity, regardless of whether or not another person participates directly in it, is also a significant form of healing. Creative action involves bonding with the world from one's own autonomous and spontaneous subjectivity (Fromm, 1947/2007a), and is both cause and consequence of the sufficient integration of the true self, as well as of its unfolding (Winnicott, 1986/2011a), apart from being a form of alchemy for emotional distress. No matter how small, the creative act brings something to the world. In that form of self-transcendence (Frankl, 1946/2013), the person leaves themselves to realize something in the world; they enrich it, and, in doing so, they enrich themselves in the revitalization of their being-in-the-world. Ideally, we refer here to actions that are not loaded with great demands and arise spontaneously from the person, but they can also be accompanied in their initiation. This implicit relational work, which strengthens the self in its reconnection with the world, will be profoundly beneficial for the disposition to bond with other people.

Returning again to Cecilia's case, we may mention how during conversations in therapy, she remembered how much she enjoyed cooking with her grandmother as a child. With some encouragement from the therapist, she made it a point to return to cooking every now and then for some family gathering. She began to do it on her own, and the results surprised her, to the point of discovering and appreciating a capacity of her own that she was unaware of. At the time of writing, on weekends Cecilia usually bakes cakes or cookies. Not only does she share them with her mother and cousin, but they are also a good excuse to visit her grandmother, even for a few minutes, and shorten the social distance they have been forced to maintain for so long. The results are not always so obvious, but there is a vitality that creative action brings every time, as long as it is not tarnished by result-oriented demands.

The inclusion of virtuality, especially social media in its capacity to foster human bonds, can be of great benefit when used with responsibility, limits, and clear purposes. It may constitute a form of transitional space, as we have said, and, at the same time, in cognitive-behavioral terms it could be thought of as an exposure technique that is in an intermediate shade between those produced in guided imagery and those that are live because one is communicating with a real person, but with technology that mediates and "softens" that contact. However, when in contact with someone real, exposure is only one aspect of what occurs, which refers to the specifically symptomatic; on a deeper level, it involves the relational—the bonding patterns and the spontaneity or falseness of the self in them. Hence, we consider Winnicott's concept of transitional space to be more complete, even for those who can consciously integrate this root concept within the framework of a progressive exposition.

It is worth adding the importance of the human faculty of acceptance with respect to oneself and to others. The practice of promoting mindfulness through its various forms of meditation has also proven effective for the specific clinical condition of social anxiety (Fernández-Álvarez & Bogiaizian, 2008). On an individual level, mindfulness trains the capacity to accept one's own thoughts, emotions, and limitations, which, paradoxically, leads to their flexibility. On a broader scale, the acceptance of existence brought on by the practice of mindfulness involves getting in touch with one's compassion, which is the loving gaze toward others and toward oneself; and, in this way, it leads to getting in touch with common humanity (Varela et al., 1991/2011; Reynoso, 2017). By working on a deep acceptance, the person unfolds the core of the bond: the connection with all the others that inhabit me as humanity and my presence in it and in all the others that make it up. It will be necessary to find a way to achieve the cultivation of this presence in each particular situation—individual, group, or collective. However, both from its practice and its paradigm, mindfulness can be very useful to disarticulate the roots of cyberbullying, social anxiety, and, mainly, of the contemporary tendency to bond disconnection.

In a similar, yet complementary way, Schneider's existential-integrative psychology (2008/2015; Segafredo, 2019) proposes the importance of being as present as possible in front of our various aspects, or of some situation in which we have been involved, that generates discomfort, rejection, or fear. Register the thoughts, emotions, and sensations they arouse. Integrate these experiences, even if we later make decisions that lead us to change them, in search and construction of a paradoxical self (integrating and balancing its different expansive and constrictive aspects), instead of stiffening within a polarized mind. This promotes untying the knots in the bonds with oneself, with others, and the world, which are inseparable, as explained by Buber and Heidegger from philosophy, Winnicott and Bowlby from psychology, and as summarized by existential psychology.

The forms of cyberbullying and social isolation (beyond that decreed by governments) have increased during the pandemic and seem to reflect a trend of disconnection from the other (and, thus, from oneself). But they also involve an appeal to deploy and strengthen our existential faculties. Likewise, the possibility of revaluing human bonds due to the limitations and lack of emotionally bonding encounters has arisen from the pandemic, which we have taken for granted throughout our lives. This is the paradox of the world's relational existence after the pandemic.

Epilogue

Hacking Automatism with Bonds, Awareness, and Meaning

"I don't know the future. I didn't come here to tell you how this is going to end. I came here to tell you how it's going to begin. Where we go from there is a choice I leave to you." Neo (Matrix)

"He shall once again behold his friends." Homer (The Odyssey)

As we venture into uncharted waters in the wake of the crisis and the extreme technologization of life brought on by the pandemic, we can always find a compass and existential nourishment in the love and encounter of our significant bonds, in the meaning to be realized, and in the expansion of the awareness of our freedom in context. This applies to the fear generated by the abyss of the crisis, as well as to the automatism that entices us with virtual everyday life and the illusory return to "normality" and, fundamentally, to the disorientation that distresses us even when we commit ourselves to the creation of new paths.

Since the beginning of the human adventure, we have been looking for clues on how to face life and its crises in our great stories. At different temporal extremes in our culture, we find the story of Neo in the Matrix and that of Ulysses, the seafarer. Neo faces a world where technology has become an end in itself and humans a means to its accomplishment. People are numbed and objectified by machines in an illusory reality, and the few who awaken are called upon to reconstruct meaning from the end of the previous world. Ulysses, on his part, is the archetype of the traveler transformed by a sudden journey into the unknown. His only guide and the source of his strength in the face of constant uncertainty are his loved ones, calling to him from Ithaca.

Every meaningful journey involves a transformation. Many of the changes we face at this time as humanity, collectively and individually contained in each of us, are already irreversible. Our relationship with the world, with others, and with ourselves has changed in every dimension of the bio-psychosocial-spiritual gestalt that we are, impacted by the pandemic and technology. Possibly in the future, this may even have neuronal consequences. Our subjectivity has changed in a kind of underlining of the impermanence of being. The opportunity to which we ascribe in this essay is learning to be the protagonists in our becoming, as people and as humanity, in this new context of face-to-face and virtual hybridization. That is, to build a way of living committed to what we value most in the deployment of our existential resources and with the necessary inclusion of technology as a means of encounter and meaning. Humanize technology, not turn the person into a machine.

The expansion of awareness in the integration of the technological dimension into our lives, with respect to existence itself, may involve the analogy of transforming the algorithm. Not leaving it on automatic, as it is configured by default on a device, on a platform, in an app, or in a social network, but to choose. Connecting and bonding based on what makes sense to you (which involves asking yourself first), in a commitment and responsibility that can be explored through technology and limiting it as well. Choosing to choose, as opposed to the comfortable but subtly restrictive technological automatism. Also choosing when to delegate something to technology and when not to. Choosing when to experience from virtuality and when to take a break from it and have fully present experiences. In the science fiction metaphor, we see the case of Neo, who learns to enter and exit the Matrix and even to add resources from that reality without alienating himself in it and with a meaning to be realized.

Choosing how we relate to ourselves, to others, and to the world, which today includes technology, builds our way of being. In concrete, everyday examples, deciding whether or not to have our entertainment content continue streaming indefinitely as a succession of episodes of a television series; whether or not to have notifications from various social networks interrupting what we do constantly throughout the day; whether or not to participate in the chain of forwarding and viralizing content that trivializes the pain of others. In the succession of examples, automation moves from the external platform to internalization, where we ourselves maintain it and objectify ourselves as just another piece of this mechanical and dehumanizing configuration. Something similar happens in everyday automatism, where one can continue doing the same thing even if it does not generate well-being or subjective growth due to the security and comfort of what's been pre-established (e.g., based on social or family mandates). This occurs on a personal and global scale. Paradoxically, the pandemic has slowed down the everyday mechanical scaffolding, but it has also imbued us with virtuality, which in turn poses additional risks of automation.

We have also seen how the bulk of the questions raised by the pandemic is related to emotional bonds and the capacity for encounter. We discovered that our bodies are connected, from China to Argentina, and our experiences and emotions have also synchronized in an unprecedented simultaneous global crisis. The oxymoron of the times is that we experience the other as a risk of contagion and also as a loved one we long to see. The contradictory experiences of "hell is other people" and "all life is encounter—as existentialist philosophers Sartre and Buber, respectively, have written—take on new meaning and depth. To approach or to move away (which also contains the classic Shakespearean question of "to be or not to be"): That seems to have been the question. And technology managed to generate a third (transitional) space, where we are in a way both far away and close. Our relational existence, the bonding of being (including our unavoidable relationship with nature) has been evidenced as rarely before. Psychologist and existential thinker Martínez Robles (Segafredo, 2021) describes it as follows:

> There is an awareness of the importance of our person-to-person bonds. I see it in my patients, my students, in myself; I miss giving my friends a hug, being with them at a barbecue, interacting in a playful way. Because we took it for granted before, it didn't seem like something we had to make decisions about. Now, by contrast, we do. I have a few patients who say, 'You know what? I can't Zoom. Can we meet in person?' And that's when I have to make a decision, because there is a risk and also a benefit. In the past, that's how we did it. Now, I have to choose. So, it leads me to something deeply existential: I am more aware that I can choose how to relate to others.

We can say that the pandemic winds have thrown us into an odyssey, where the oceans of the physical and the virtual presence intersect, hiding existential riches to be discovered and created, but also a kind of Matrix, just waiting for us to slip up. There are several dangers in this navigation: the hypnotic chants of narcissism and inauthenticity that come from the individualism, the addiction to success and neoconsumerism of the digital society; the drowsiness and forgetfulness of presence in one's own life due to the problematic and addictive consumption of connection; the possibility of being swallowed by an aggravated violence and distance with the other, manifested in cyberbullying, objectification, and marginalization; as well as the vortex of anguish to which the current of uncertainty may lead us, if we passively navigate it.

In a new paradox, we may understand this as a journey into the unknown and, at the same time, into our own humanity. The unfolding and rediscovery of our existential–spiritual resources of acceptance, meaning, creativity, and encounter that this journey awakens may mean "coming home," even in the creation of a new one. In fact, the situation urges us toward a renewed contextualized planetary humanism in the contemporary pandemic and post-pandemic world. This includes promotion, prevention, treatment, and recovery in mental health, which can no longer omit the spiritual and existential dimension of life (which contains the other) but extends much further, on a social, community, and planetary scale. The current crisis clearly shows the becoming of existence and the inexorable link between person–society–planet, whose various levels are contained and co-constructed as in a fractal.

There are no clear answers for everything we will come across on this journey, or how to solve each of the problems it will bring, or when it will end (so that another one can begin). However, there are clues on how to learn to navigate existence and its storms. Today these include entering and exiting the virtual Matrix and crossing the abyss of uncertainty on a daily basis, with the compass of our awareness, meaning, and emotional bonds. To return to the bonding, to affection, to the encounter, to our common humanity (which involves appreciating and transcending the closest bonds), to build new meanings based on awareness and commitment to what we value most, individually and collectively. To transcend horizons while returning to ourselves. To awaken our humanity in order to be the protagonist in its becoming—from the microcosm of daily life and personal projects to the macrocosm of the community and the planet.

References

Aguiar, A., Pinto, M., & Duarte, R. (2020). Grief and mourning during the COVID-19 pandemic in Portugal. *Acta Medica Portuguesa, 33*(9), 543–545. https://doi.org/10.20344/AMP.14345

Agus, M., Mascia, M. L., Zanetti, M. A., Perrone, S., Rollo, D., & Penna, M.P. (2021). Who are the victims of cyberbullying? Preliminary data towards validation of cyberbullying victim questionnaire. *Contemporary Educational Technology, 13*(3), Article ep310. https://doi.org/10.30935/cedtech/10888

Alomo, M., Gagliardi, G., Peloche, S., Somers, E., Alzina, P., & Prokopez, C. R. (2020). Efectos psicológicos de la pandemia COVID-19 en la población general de Argentina. [Psychological effects of the COVID-19 pandemic on the general population of Argentina]. *Revista de la Facultad de Ciencias Médicas de Córdoba, 77*(3), 176–181. https://doi.org/10.31053/1853.0605.v77.n3.28561

Alonso, M. P. (2011). Trastornos del control de los impulsos [Impulse control disorders]. In J. Vallejo Ruiloba (Ed.), *Introducción a la psicopatología y la psiquiatría* [Introduction to psychopathology and psychiatry] (7th ed., pp. 385–399).

American Academy of Arts & Sciences. (2020). *Sherry Turkle: Technology and empathy after Covid-19* [Video]. YouTube. https://www.youtube.com/watch?v=DqjqcB9GjxA

American Psychiatric Association (2016). *Manual diagnóstico y estadístico de los trastornos mentales* [Diagnostic and statistical manual of mental disorders] (5th. ed.). Editorial Médica Panamericana.

Andreassen, C.S., Pallesen, S., & Griffiths, M.D. (2017). The relationship between addictive use of social media, narcissism, and self-esteem: Findings from a large national survey. *Addictive Behaviors, 64*, 287–293. https://doi.org/10.1016/j.addbeh.2016.03.006

Arrivillaga, C., Rey, L., & Extremera, N. (2020). Perfil emocional de adolescentes en riesgo de un uso problemático de internet [Emotional profile of adolescents at risk of problematic internet use]. *Revista de Psicología Clínica con Niños y Adolescentes, 8*(1), 47–53. https://www.revistapcna.com/sites/default/files/6.pdf

Ansary, N.S. (2020). Cyberbullying: Concepts, theories, and correlates informing evidence-based best practises for prevention. *Aggression and Violent Behavior, 50*, Article 101343. https://doi.org/10.1016/j.avb.2019.101343

Anzieu, D. (1998). *El Yo-piel* [The skin-ego] (3rd ed.; S. Vidarrazaga Zimmermann, Trans). Biblioteca Nueva.

Asmundson, G. J. G., & Taylor, S. (2020). Coronaphobia: Fear and the 2019-nCoV outbreak. *Journal of Anxiety Disorders, 70*, Article 102196. https://doi.org/10.1016/j.janxdis.2020.102196

Baeza Velasco, C. (2007). Tratamientos eficaces para el Trastorno de Ansiedad Social [Effective treatments for social anxiety disorder]. *Cuaernosd. Neuropsicol., 1*(2), 127–138.

Bados López, A., & García Grau, E. (2011). *Técnicas de Exposición* [Exposure Techniques]. Departamento de Personalidad, Evaluación y Tratamiento Psicológicos, Facultad de Psicología, Universidad de Barcelona. http://diposit.ub.edu/dspace/bitstream/2445/18403/1/T%C3%A9cnic as%20de%20Exposici%C3%B3n%202011.pdf

Bäuerle, A., Teufel, M., Musche, V., Weismüller, B., Kohler, H., Hetkamp, M., Dörrie, N., Schweda, A., & Skoda, E. M. (2020). Increased generalised anxiety, depression and distress during the COVID-19 pandemic: A cross-sectional study in Germany. *Journal of Public Health, 42*(4), 672–678. https://doi.org/10.1093/pubmed/fdaa106

Bauman, Z. (2018). *Amor líquido, sobre la fragilidad de los vínculos humanos* [Liquid love, On the frailty of human bonds] (A. Santos Mosquera, Trans.). Editorial Paidós. (Original work published 2003).

BBC News Mundo (2021, March 18). "Hay mucho miedo": Por qué han aumentado los ataques contra miembros de la comunidad asiática en EE.UU. ["There is a lot of fear": Why have attacks against members of the Asian community in the US increased?]. https://www.bbc.com/mundo/noticias-internacional-56423587

Beck, U. (2005). *La mirada cosmopolita o la guerra es la paz* [The cosmopolitan perspective or war is peace] (B. Moreno Carrillo, Trans.). Editorial Paidós.

Bilinkis, S. (2019). *Guía para sobrevivir al presente* [Guide to survive the present]. Sudamericana.

Blinka, L., Sablatúrová, N., Sevcíková, A., & Husarova, D. (2020). Social constraints associated with excessive internet use in adolescents: The role of family, school, peers, and neighbourhood. *International Journal of Public Health, 65*, 1279–1287. https://doi.org/10.1007/s00038-020-01462-8

Blustein, D. L., & Guarino, P. A. (2020). Work and unemployment in the time of COVID-19: The existential experience of loss and fear. *Journal of Humanistic Psychology, 60*(5), 702–709. https://doi.org/10.1177/0022167820934229

Bonavitta, P. (2015). El amor en los tiempos de Tinder [Love in times of tinder]. *Cultura y representaciones sociales,10*(19), 157–210. http://www.scielo.org.mx/scielo.php?script=sci_arttext&pid=S2007-81102015000200009&lng=es&tlng=es

Bowlby, J. (2012). *El apego* [Attachment] (M. Valcarce Avello, Trans.). Editorial Paidós. (Original work published 1969).

Bowlby, J. (1998), *La separación* [Separation] (I. Pardal, Trans.). Editorial Paidós. (Original work published 1973)

Brailovsky, D. (2020). *"Caer" en la educación virtual* [To fall into virtual education]. Panorama OEI Portal a la Educación. https://panorama.oei.org.ar/caer-en-la-educacion-virtual/

Brewer, G., & Kerslake, J. (2015). Cyberbullying, self-esteem, empathy and loneliness. *Computers in Human Behavior*, 48, 255–260. https://doi.org/10.1016/j.chb.2015.01.073

Bugental, J. (2008). Niveles ónticos del crecimiento terapéutico [Ontic levels in therapeutic growth] (M. Guastavino, Trans.). In Walsh, R., & Vaughan, F. (Eds.), *Más allá del ego* [Paths beyond ego] (10th ed., pp. 294–302). Editorial Kairós. (Original work published 1980).

Buber, M. (2013). *Yo y Tú* [I and thou]. Prometeo libros. (Original work published in 1923).

Buomprisco, G., Ricci, S., Perri, R., & De Sio, S. (2021). Health and telework: New challenges after COVID-19 pandemic. *European Journal of Environment and Public Health*, 5(2), Article em0073. https://doi.org/10.21601/ejeph/9705

Casas, M., Duro, P., & Pinet, C. (2011). Otras drogodependencias [Other drug addictions]. In J. Vallejo Ruiloba (Ed.), *Introducción a la psicopatología y la psiquiatría* [Introduction to psychopathology and psychiatry] (7th ed., pp. 359–384). Elsevier Masson.

Chakraborty, S., Bhattacherjee, A., & Onuchowska, A. (2021, March 9). Cyberbullying: A review of the literature. *Social Science Research Network (SSRN)*. http://dx.doi.org/10.2139/ssrn.3799920

Cerniglia, L., Zoratto, F., Cimino, S., Laviola, G., Ammaniti, M., & Adriani, W. (2017). Internet addiction in adolescence: Neurobiological, psychosocial and clinical issues. *Neuroscience and Biobehavioral Reviews*, 76, 174–184. http://dx.doi.org/10.1016/j.neubiorev.2016.12.024

Cheng, C., & Yee-Lam Li, A. (2014). Internet addiction prevalence and quality of (real) life: A meta-analysis of 31 nations across seven world regions. *Cyberpsychology, behavior and social networking*, 17(12), 755–760. https://doi.org/10.1089/cyber.2014.0317

Conangla, M. (2002). *Crisis Emocionales* [Emotional Crisis]. Amat editorial.

Conrad, R., Forstner, A. J., Chung, M. L., Mücke, M., Geiser, F., Schumacher, J., & Carnehl, F. (2021). Significance of anger suppression and preoccupied attachment in social anxiety disorder: A cross-sectional study. *BMC Psychiatry*, 21, Article 116. https://doi.org/10.1186/s12888-021-03098-1

Damasio, A. (2014). *En busca de Spinoza* [Looking for Spinoza] (J. Ros, Trans.). Editorial Paidós. (Original work published 2003)

De Sousa, F. (2021). A new and old pandemic – The burnout syndrome. *MOJ Gerontology & Geriatrics*, 6(1), 22–26. http://doi.org/10.15406/mojgg.2021.06.00262

Del Prete, A., & Redon Pantoja, S. (2020). Las redes sociales virtuales: Espacios de socialización y definición de identidad [Online social

networks: Spaces for socialization and definition of identity].
Psicoperspectivas, 19(1), 1–11.
http://dx.doi.org/10.5027/psicoperspectivas-vol19-issue1-fulltext-1834

Dresp, B. (2020). Internet Addiction Disorder (IAD). In E*ncyclopedia, section on psychiatry and mental health studies*. https://encyclopedia.pub/1338

Durao, M. (2017). *Análisis del impacto del uso de videollamadas en el ejercicio de la psicoterapia: la perspectiva de los terapeutas* [Analysis of the impact of the use of video calls in psychotherapy: Therapists' perspective] (Publication No. 19577) [Doctoral Thesis, Universidad de Flores]. ABCD On Line / Winisis On Line. http://www.abcdonline.com.ar/uflo/

Durao, M. (2021, March 30) Mindfulness y tecnología 3 preguntas a Martin (Reynosos [Mindfulness and technology: 3 questions to Martin Reynoso). [Video]. Instagram. Retrieved from https://www.insatgram.com/tv/CND765PHWbk/?unt_medium+copy_li

Eguiluz, I., & Segarra, R. (2017). *Introducción a la Psicopatología* [Introduction to psychopathology]. Editorial Médica Panamericana.

Erikson, E. (1987). *Childhood and society.* Paladin Grafton Books. (Original work published 1950)

Ettman, C.K., Abdalla, S.M., Cohen, G.H., Sampson, L., Vivier, P. M., & Galea, S. (2020). Prevalence of depression symptoms in US adults before and during the COVID-19 pandemic. *JAMA Network Open, 3*(9), Article e2019686. http://doi.org/10.1001/jamanetworkopen.2020.19686

Feijóo, S., Foody, M., O'Higgins Norman, J., Pichel, R., & Rial, A. (2021). Cyberbullies, the cyberbullied, and problematic internet use: Some reasonable similarities. *Psicothema, 33*(2), 198–205. http://doi.org/10.7334/psicothema2020.209

Fernández-Álvarez, H., & Bogiazian, D. (2008). *El miedo a los otros, Avances en el tratamiento de la fobia social* [Fear of others, Advances in the treatment of social phobia]. Lumen.

Fernández Mouján, O. (1999). *Crisis vital, un modelo de transformación en psicoanálisis y psicología social* [Vital Crisis, a Model of transformation in psychoanalysis and social psychology]. Editorial Nueva Visión.

Fox, M. (2020, July 28). Remote work burnout is growing as pandemic stretches on. Here's how to manage it. *CNBC.* https://www.cnbc.com/2020/07/28/remote-work-burnout-is-growing-as-coronavirus-pandemic-stretches-on.html

Frankl, V. (1986). *El hombre en busca de sentido* [Man's search for meaning] (Gorki, Trans.). Editorial Herder. (Original work published 1946)

Frankl, V. (2003). *Ante el vacío existencial, hacia una humanización de la psicoterapia* [Facing existential emptiness, Towards a humanization of psychotherapy] (M. Villanueva, Trans.). Editorial Herder. (Original work published 1977)

Frankl, V. (2013). *Psicoanálisis y existencialismo* [Psychoanalysis and existentialism (2nd ed.; C. Silva, & J. Mendoza, Trans.). Fondo de Cultura Económica. (Original work published 1946)

Frankl, V. (2014). *Psicoterapia y humanismo, ¿Tiene un sentido la vida?* [Psychotherapy and humanism, Does life have a meaning?] (2nd ed.) (A. Guéra Miralles, Trans.). Fondo de Cultura Económica. (Original work published 1978)

Freud, S. (1993). Introducción del narcisismo [On narcissism: An introduction]. In Freud, S., *Obras completas, Vol. 14: Contribución a la historia del movimiento psicoanalítico. Trabajos sobre metapsicología y otras obras.* [Complete works, Vol. 14: Contribution to the history of the psychoanalytic movement. Works on Metapsychology and other works.] (2nd ed., pp. 65–98) (J. L. Etcheverry, Trans.). Amorrortu Editores. (Original work published 1914)

Fromm, E. (2007a). *El miedo a la libertad* [The fear of freedom (3rd ed.; G. Germani, Trans.). Editorial Paidós. (Original work published 1947)

Fromm, E. (2007b). *El humanismo como utopía real* [Humanism as a realistic utopia] (E. Fuente Herrero, , Trans.). Editorial Paidós.

Futures of Education International Commission. (2020). *La educación en un mundo tras la COVID: Nueve ideas para la acción pública* [Education in a post-COVID world: Nine ideas for public action]. UNESCO. https://unesdoc.unesco.org/ark:/48223/pf0000373717_spa

Gardner, H. (2011). *La inteligencia reformulada, las inteligencias múltiples en el siglo XXI* [Reformulated intelligence, multiple intelligences in the 21st century] (G. Sánchez Barberán, Trans.). Editorial Paidós. (Original work published 1999)

Gewin, V. (2021). Pandemic burnout is rampant in academia. *Nature, 591*, 489–491. https://doi.org/10.1038/d41586-021-00663-2

Gil, F., del Valle, G., Oberst, U., & Chamarro, A. (2015). Nuevas tecnologías - ¿Nuevas patologías? El smartphone y el fear of missing out [New technologies - New pathologies? The smartphone and the fear of missing out]. *Aloma, Revista de Psicologia, Ciències de l'Eduació i de l'Esport, 33*(2), 77–83. https://doi.org/10.51698/aloma.2015.33.2.77-83

Gil-Or, O., Levi-Belz, Y., & Turel, O. (2015). The "Facebook-self": Characteristics and psychological predictors of false self-presentation on Facebook. *Frontiers in Psychology, 6*, Article 99. https://doi.org/10.3389/fpsyg.2015.00099

Goleman, D. (2009). *Inteligencia ecológica* [Ecological intelligence] (D. González Raga, Trans.). Editorial Kairós.

Gorman, T.E., & Green, C.S. (2016). Short-term mindfulness intervention reduces the negative attentional effects associated with heavy media multitasking. *Scientific Reports, 6*, Article 24542. https://doi.org/10.1038/srep24542

Grant, A. (2021, April 21). There's a name for the blah you're feeling: It's called languishing. *The New York Times.* https://www.nytimes.com/2021/04/19/well/mind/covid-mental-health-languishing.html

Halpern, D., & Valenzuela, S. (2016). "Selfie-ists" or "Narci-selfiers"?: A cross-lagged panel analysis of selfie taking and narcissism. *Personality and Individual Differences, 97*, 98–101.
https://doi.org/10.1016/j.paid.2016.03.019.

Han, B.-C. (2020). La emergencia viral y el mundo del mañana [Viral Emergency and tomorrow 's world]. In P. Amadeo (Ed.), *Sopa de Wuhan, pensamiento contemporáneo en tiempos de pandemia* [Wuhan soup, Contemporary thinking in times of pandemic] (pp. 97–11). ASPO.
https://www.perio.unlp.edu.ar/catedras/hdelconocimiento/wp-content/uploads/sites/129/2020/04/Sopa-de-Wuhan-ASPO_copy.pdf

Han, B.-C. (2019). *La expulsión de lo distinto, percepción y comunicación en la sociedad actual* [The expulsion of the other, Perception and communication today] (A. Ciria, Trans.). Editorial Herder. (Original work published 2016)

Heidegger, M. (2018). *El ser y el tiempo* [Being and time] (2nd. ed.; J. Gaos, Trans.). Fondo de Cultura Económica. (Original work published 1927)

Hirsch, H., & Durao, M. (2020). *Psicoterapia online, qué es y cómo se practica* [Online psychotherapy, What it is and how it is practiced]. Centro Privado de Psicoterapia.

Hussain, Z., & Pontes, H.M. (2019). Personality, internet addiction, and other technological addictions: A psychological examination of personality traits and technological addictions. In M. Khosrow-Pour (Ed.), *Substance abuse and addiction: Breakthroughs in research and practice* (pp. 45–71). IGI Global.

International Labour Organization. (2020a). *La COVID-19 y el mundo del trabajo.* [COVID-19 and the world of work] (6th ed.). https://www.ilo.org/wcmsp5/groups/public/---dgreports/---dcomm/documents/briefingnote/wcms_755917.pdf

International Labour Organization. (2020b). *Impactos en el mercado del trabajo y los ingresos en América Latina y el Caribe* [Impacts on the Labor Market and Income in Latin America and the Caribbean] (2nd ed.). https://www.ilo.org/wcmsp5/groups/public/---americas/---ro-lima/documents/publication/wcms_756694.pdf

Jain, O., Gupta, M., Satam, S., & Panda, S. (2020). Has the COVID-19 pandemic affected the susceptibility to cyberbullying in India? *Computers in Human Behavior Reports, 2*, Article 100029.
https://doi.org/10.1016/j.chbr.2020.100029

Jaspers, K. (2012). *Psicopatologia generale* [General psychopathology] (7th ed.; R. Priori, Trans.). Il pensiero scientifico editore. (Original work published 1913)

Jaspers, K. (1950). *Psicologia delle visioni del mondo* [Psychology of Worldviews] (V. Loriga, Trans.). Casa Editrice Astrolabio. (Original work published 1919)

Kabat-Zinn, J. (2016). *Vivir con plenitud las crisis* [Full catastrophe living] (A. de Satrústegui, Trans.). Editorial Kairós. (Original work published 1990)

Kierkegaard, S. (2007). *Tratado de la desesperación* [Treatise on despair] (F. Cardozo, Trans.) Editorial Gradifco. (Original work published 1849)

Kohut, H. (1980). *La restauración del sí mismo* [The restoration of the self] (N. Rosenblatt, Trans.). Editorial Paidós. (Original work published 1977)

Kontoangelos, K., Economou, M., & Papageorgiou, C. (2020). Mental health effects of COVID-19 Pandemic: A review of clinical and psychological traits. *Psychiatry Investigation, 17*(6), 491–505. https://doi.org/10.30773/pi.2020.0161

Kübler-Ross, E., & Kessler, D. (2018). *Sobre el duelo y el dolor* [On grief and grieving] (S. Gulu Navarro, Trans.) Editorial Oniro. (Original work published 2005)

Lipovetsky, G. (2014). *La era del vacío* [The empty era] (12th ed.; M. Pendanx, & J. Vinyoli Sastre, Trans.). Editorial Anagrama. (Original work published 1983)

Lottridge, D., Rosakranse, C., Oh, C., Westwood, S., Baldoni, K., Mann, A., & Nass, C. (2015). The effects of chronic multitasking on analytical writing. in special interest group on computer-human interaction. *CHI '15: Proceedings of the 33rd Annual ACM Conference on Human Factors in Computing Systems* (pp. 2967–2970). https://doi.org/10.1145/2702123.2702367

Luo, M., Guo, L., Yu, M., Jiang, W., & Wang, H. (2020). The psychological and mental impact of coronavirus disease 2019 (COVID-19) on medical staff and general public - A systematic review and meta-analysis. *Psychiatry Research, 291*, Article 113190. https://doi.org/10.1016/j.psychres.2020.113190

March, E., & McBean, T. (2018). New evidence shows self-esteem moderates the relationship between narcissism and selfies. *Personality and Individual Differences*, 130, 107-111. https://doi.org/10.1016/j.paid.2018.03.053

Marian Durao PhD [@mariandurao_psy]. (2021, March 30). *Mindfullnes y tecnología 3 preguntas a Martín Reynoso* [Mindfulness and technology: 3 questions to Martín Reynoso] [Video]. Instagram. https://www.instagram.com/tv/CND765PHWbk/?utm_medium=copy_link

Maritchu Seitun [@maritchuseitun]. (2020, August 4).Charla de juego y tecnología en cuarentena @maritchuseitun y Sofi Chas @cuentosyjuegosparacrecer [talk on games and technology in quarantine; Video]. Instagram. https://www.instagram.com/tv/CDef0kij-KG/?hl=es

Marques de Miranda, D., da Silva Athanasio, B., Sena Oliveira, C., & Simoes-e-Silva, A. C. (2020). How is COVID-19 pandemic impacting mental health of children and adolescents? *International Journal of Disaster Risk Reduction, 51*, Article 101845. https://doi.org/10.1016/j.ijdrr.2020.101845

Marra e Rosa, G. A., Rodrigues dos Santos, B., Stengel, M., & de Freitas, M. H. (2016). Estetización del self en redes sociales: contradicciones humanas y producción subjetiva contemporánea [Aestheticization of the aelf in social Networks: Human contradictions and contemporary subjective production]. *Revista de Psicología, 34*(2), 313–336. http://dx.doi.org/10.18800/psico.201602.004

Marrone, M. (2009). *La teoría del apego, un enfoque actual* [Attachment Theory, a Contemporary Approach]. Editorial Psimática.

Martínez Ortiz, E. (2009). Modelo logoterapéutico-ambulatorio en adicciones [Outpatient-logotherapeutic model in addictions]. In S. Sáenz Valiente, (Ed.), *Logoterapia en acción, aplicaciones prácticas* [Logotherapy in action, practical applications] (pp. 435–450). Editorial San Pablo.

Martínez Ortiz, E., Castellanos, C., Osorio Castaño, C.A., & Camacho Lee, S. (2015). Efectos de la logoterapia sobre los recursos personales de las personas con adicción [Effects of logotherapy on the personal resources of people with addiction]. *Revista Argentina de Clínica Psicológica, 24*(3), 231–241.

Martínez Robles, Y. (2012). *Psicoterapia existencial, teoría y práctica relacional para un mundo post-cartesiano* [Existential psychotherapy, relational theory and practice for a post-Cartesian world]. Diana Reyes Trigos.

Maslow, A. H. (2012). *El hombre autorrealizado, hacia una psicología del ser* [The self-actualized man, Towards a psychology of being] (19th ed.; (R. Ribé, Trans.). Editorial Kairós. (Original work published 1962)

May, R. (1987). *La psicología y el dilema del hombre* [Psychology and the human dilemma] (D. Ares, & M. Wald, Trans.). Editorial Gedisa. (Original work published 1967)

May, R. (Ed.). (1991). *Existential psychology* (2nd ed.). McGraw-Hill Inc. (Original work published 1961)

May, R. (1994). *The courage to create.* Bantam Books. (Original work published 1975)

Mazzulla, M. M., & Gómez, B. (2011). Abordaje de trastornos emocionales [Approaching emotional disorders]. In H. Fernández Álvarez, (Ed.), *Paisajes de la psicoterapia* [Psychotherapy landscapes] (pp. 191–214). Editorial Polemos.

Méndez, M. (2020). Hoy lo vivo está en mirar la muerte: Información y alienación en la era de la pandemia [Today´s life is in looking at death: Information and alienation in the era of the pandemic]. *Ensayos de Filosofía, 12*, Article 2. https://doi.org/10.13140/RG.2.2.18572.13441

Mitchell, S. (2018). *Gli orientamenti relazionali in psicoanalisi, per un modello integrato* [Relational concepts in psychoanalysis: An integration] (S. Rivolta, Trans.). Bollati Boringhieri Editore. (Original work published 1988)

Moon, J. H., Lee, E., Lee, J. A., Choi, T. R., & Sung, Y. (2016). The role of narcissism in self-promotion on Instagram. *Personality and Individual Differences, 101*, 22–25. https://doi.org/10.1016/j.paid.2016.05.042

Morin, E. (1993). *Tierra patria* [Homeland earth] (R. Figueira, Trans.). Nueva Visión.

Morin, E. (1999). *Los siete saberes necesarios para la educación del futuro* [Seven lessons in education for the future] (M. Vallejo-Gómez, Trans.). UNESCO.

Morin, E. (2010). *¿Hacia el abismo? Globalización en el siglo XXI* [Into the abyss? Globalization in the 21st century] (A. M. Malaina Martin, Trans.). Editorial Paidós (Original work published 2007)

Morin, E. (2020). *Cambiemos de vía, lecciones de la pandemia* [Let 's change our way, Lessons of the pandemic] (N. Petit Fontseré, Trans.). Editorial Paidós.

Oro, O. R. (2016). *Persona y personalidad* [Person and Personality]. Fundación Argentina de Logoterapia.

Öztürk, A., & Mutlu, T. (2010). The relationship between attachment style, subjective well-being, happiness and social anxiety among university students. *Procedia Social and Behavioral Sciences, 9*, 1772–1776. https://doi.org/10.1016/j.sbspro.2010.12.398

Palumbo, M. (2019). Búsquedas de vínculos eróticos y/o afectivos a través de las apps. Un estudio comparado entre la Ciudad de Buenos Aires y la Ciudad de México [Searches for erotic and/or affective relationships through apps. A comparative study between the City of Buenos Aires and Mexico City]. *Revista Mora, 25*, 155–172. https://doi.org/10.34096/mora.n25.8527

Perel, E., & Miller, M. A. (2020). Feeling alone in a relationship? You're not alone. *Letters from Esther.* https://www.estherperel.com/blog/feeling-alone-in-a-relationship-youre-not-alone

Piaget, J., & Inhelder, B. (2015). *Psicología del niño* [The psychology of the child] (18th ed.; J. Delval, & P. Lomeli, Trans.). Ediciones Morata. (Original work published 1969)

Pietromonaco, P. R., & Overall, N. C. (2021). Applying relationship science to evaluate how the COVID-19 pandemic may impact couples' relationships. *American Psychologist, 76*(3), 438–450. http://dx.doi.org/10.1037/amp0000714

Reloba, S., Chirosa, L. J., & Reigal, R.E. (2016). Relación entre actividad física, procesos cognitivos y rendimiento académico de escolares: revisión de la literatura actual [Relationship between physical activity, cognitive processes and academic performance of schoolchildren: A review of the current literature]. *Revista Andaluza de Medicina del Deporte, 9*(4), 166–172. https://dx.doi.org/10.1016/j.ramd.2015.05.008

Reynoso, M. (2017). *Mindfulness, la meditación científica* [Mindfulness, the scientific meditation]. Editorial Paidós.

Reynoso, M. (2020, April 30). 7 consejos para disminuir la 'fatiga de la empatía' por las videollamadas en cuarentena [Seven recommendations to diminish video call "empathy fatigue" in quarantine]. *Diario Clarín.* https://www.clarin.com/buena-vida/7-consejos-disminuir-fatiga-empatia-videollamadas-cuarentena_0_sP-Bp-kvr.html

Rogers, C. (1989). *La terapia centrata-sul-cliente* [Client-centered therapy] (F. Carugati, M. Magistretti, T. Montevecchi, A. Palmonari, & P. Ricci-Bitti, Trans.). Martinelli & Co. (Original work published 1951)

Romera, E. M., Camacho, A., Ortega-Ruiz, R., & Falla, D. (2021). Cybergossip, cyberaggression, problematic Internet use and family communication. *Comunicar, 67,* 61–71. https://doi.org/10.3916/C67-2021-05

Rooksby, M., McLead, H. J., & Furuhashi, T. (2020). Hikikomori: A hidden mental health need following the COVID-19 pandemic. *World Psychiatry,* 19(3), 399–400. https://doi.org/10.1002/wps.20804

Rudnicki, K., & Steiger, S. (2020). *Online hate speech.* Detect then act, Rights, equality and citizenship programme of the European Union (2014–2020). https://dtct.eu/resources/

Ruíz-Martín, A., Bono-Cabré, R., & Magallón-Neri, E. (2019). Ciberacoso y ansiedad social en adolescentes: una revisión sistemática [Ciberbullying and social anxiety in adolescents: A systematic review]. *Revista de Psicología Clínica con Niños y Adolescentes, 6*(1), 9–15. https://doi.org/10.21134/rpcna.2019.06.1.1

Salari, N., Hosseinian-Far, A., Jalali, R., Vaisi-Raygani, A., Rasoulpoor, S., Mohammadi, M., Rasoulpoor, S., & Khaledi-Paveh, B. (2020). Prevalence of stress, anxiety, depression among the general population during the COVID-19 pandemic: A systematic review and meta-analysis. *Globalization and Health, 16,* Article 57. https://doi.org/10.1186/s12992-020-00589-w

Sartre, J. P. (2016). *El existencialismo es un humanismo* [Existentialism is a humanism] (V. Praci de Fernández, Trans.). Editorial Edhasa. (Original work published 1946)

Scherb, E. D., & Durao, M. (2017). *Tratamientos eficaces con psicoterapia integrativa* [Effective treatments with Integrative Psychotherapy]. Akadia Editorial.

Schneider, K. (Ed.). (2015). *Existential-integrative psychotherapy.* Routledge. (Original work published 2008)

Schneider, K. (2019). *The spirituality of awe: Challenges to the robotic revolution* (revised ed.). University Professors Press. (Original work published 2017)

Segafredo, G. (2019). Entrevista a Kirk Schneider [Interview with Kirk Schneider] *Revista Latinoamericana de Psicoterapia Existencial, Un Enfoque Comprensivo del Ser, 9*(19), 45–50. https://www.fundacioncapac.org.ar/revista_alpe/index.php/RLPE/articl e/view/79

Segafredo, G. (2020). Entrevista a Alfried Längle [Interview with Alfried Längle]. *Revista Latinoamericana de Psicoterapia Existencial, Un Enfoque Comprensivo del Ser*, 10(20), 39–43. https://www.fundacioncapac.org.ar/revista_alpe/index.php/RLPE/articl e/view/90

Segafredo, G. (2021). Entrevista a Susana Signorelli, Yaqui Martínez y Ramiro Gómez Salas [Interview with Susana Signorelli, Yaqui Martínez and Ramiro Gómez Salas]. *Revista Latinoamericana de Psicoterapia Existencial, Un Enfoque Comprensivo del Ser*, 11(22), 39–42. https://www.fundacioncapac.org.ar/revista_alpe/index.php/RLPE/articl e/view/116/pdf

Segafredo, G., & Durao, M. (2021). Un abordaje integrativo-existencial de las crisis vitales situacionales [An existential-integrativeapproach to situational life crisis]. *Revista Latinoamericana de Psicoterapia Existencial, Un Enfoque Comprensivo del Ser*, 12(23), 20–26. https://www.fundacioncapac.org.ar/revista_alpe/index.php/RLPE/articl e/view/122

Segal, Z., Williams, M., & Teasdale, J. (2015). *Terapia cognitiva basada en el mindfulness para la depresión* [Mindfulness-based cognitive therapy for depression] (2nd ed.) (D. González Raga, & F. Mora, Trans.). Editorial Kairós. (Original work published 2013)

Signorelli, S., Guberman, M., Abadjieff, E., Glikin, T., & Villagra, L. (2020). Sentimientos frente a la pandemia, a la cuarentena y reacciones sociales en Argentina y Latinoamérica [Feelings in the face of the Pandemic, The quarantine and social reactions in Argentina and Latin America]. *Revista Latinoamericana de Psicoterapia Existencial, Un Enfoque Comprensivo del Ser*, *10*(21), 25–37. https://www.fundacioncapac.org.ar/revista_alpe/index.php/RLPE/articl e/view/99

Sukhdeep, K., Maheshwari, S. K., & Sharma, P. (2018). Narcissistic personality and selfie taking behavior among college students. *International Journal of Medical and Health Research, 4*(5), 56–60. http://www.medicalsciencejournal.com/archives/2018/vol4/issue5/4-5-28

Sun, Y., Li, Y., Bao, Y., Meng, S., Sun, Y., Schumann, G., Kosten, T., Strang, J., Lu, L., & Shi, J. (2020). Brief report: Increased addictive internet and substance use behavior during the COVID-19 pandemic in China. *The American Journal on Addictions*, *29*, 268–270. https://doi.org/10.1111/ajad.13066

Tanconectados [@tanconectados]. (2020, September 4). *Pantallas, conductas y emociones* [Screens, behaviors and emotions] [Video]. Instagram. https://www.instagram.com/tv/CEu-XYWJElq/?utm_medium=copy_link

Thomason, B. (2021, January 26), Help your team beat WFH burnout. *Harvard Business Review*. https://hbr.org/2021/01/help-your-team-beat-wfh-burnout

Thomson, C., Mancebo, M. C., & Moitra, E. (2021). Changes in social anxiety symptoms and loneliness after increased isolation during the COVID-19 pandemic. *Psychiatry Research, 298*, Article 113834. https://doi.org/10.1016/j.psychres.2021.113834

Torres-Serrano, M. (2020). Fear of missing out (FOMO) y el uso de Instagram: Análisis de las relaciones entre narcisismo y autoestima [Fear of missing out (FOMO) and the use of Instagram: Analysis of the relationships between narcissism and self-esteem]. *Aloma, Revista de Psicologia, Ciències de l'Eduació i de l'Esport, 38*(1), 31–38. http://www.revistaaloma.net/index.php/aloma/article/view/396

Turkle, S. (2017). *Alone Together* (2nd ed.). Hachette Book Group. (Original work published 2011)

Turel, O., & Gil-Or, O. (2019). To share or not to share? The roles of false Facebook self, sex, and narcissism in re-posting self-image enhancing products. *Personality and Individual Differences, 151*, Article 109506. https://doi.org/10.1016/j.paid.2019.109506

Twenge, J. M., Konrath, S., Foster, J. D., Campbell, W. K., & Bushman, B. J. (2008). Egos inflating over time: A cross-temporal meta-analysis of the narcissistic personality inventory. *Journal of Personality, 76*(4), 875–902. https://doi.org/10.1111/j.1467-6494.2008.00507.x

Twenge, J. M., Campbell, W. K., & Gentile, B. (2012). Generational increases in agentic self-evaluations among American college students, 1966–2009. *Self and Identity, 11*(4), 409–427. https://doi.org/10.1080/15298868.2011.576820

Vallejo Ruiloba, J. (2011). Fobias [Phobias]. In J. Vallejo Ruiloba (Ed.), *Introducción a la psicopatología y la psiquiatría* [Introduction to psychopathology and psychiatry] (7th ed., pp. 155–167). Elsevier Masson.

Vallejo-Slocker, L., & Vallejo, M. A. (2016). Sobre la desensibilización sistemática, una técnica superada o renombrada [Concerning Systematic Desensitisation. An overcomed or renowned technique?]. *Acción Psicológica, 13*(2), 157–168. http://dx.doi.org/10.5944/ap.13.2.16539

van der Schuur, W. A., Baumgartner, S.E., Sumter, S.R., & Valkenburg, P. M. (2020). Exploring the long-term relationship between academic-media multitasking and adolescents' academic achievement. *New Media & Society, 22*(1), 140–158. https://doi.org/10.1177/1461444819861956

Varela, F. (2000). *El fenómeno de la vida* [The phenomenon of life] J. C. Saez (Ed).

Varela, F., Thompson, E., & Rosch, E. (2011). *De cuerpo presente, las ciencias cognitivas y la experiencia humana* [The embodied Mind, Cognitive science and human experience] (4th ed.; C. Gardini, Trans.). Editorial Gedisa. (Original work published 1991)

Vater, A., Moritz, S., & Roepke, S. (2018). Does a narcissism epidemic exist in modern western societies? Comparing narcissism and self-esteem in East

and West Germany. *PLOS ONE,* 13(1), Article e0188287.
https://doi.org/10.1371/journal.pone.0188287

Vedia Domingo, V. (2016). Duelo patológico: Factores de riesgo y protección [Pathological grief: Risk and protective factors]. *Revista Digital de Medicina Psicosomática y Psicoterapia, 6*(2), 12–34.
https://www.psicociencias.org/pdf_noticias/Duelo_patologico.pdf

Vigotsky, L. (2012). *Pensamiento y habla* [Thinking and speech] (A. A. González, Trans.). Ediciones Colihue. (Original work published 1934)

Von Boetticher, A. (2016). Deseando Conectarse [Wishing to connect]. *Revista de Psicopatología y Salud Mental en Niños y Adolescentes, 28,* 67–73.
https://www.fundacioorienta.com/wp-content/uploads/2019/02/Boeticher-A-28.pdf

We are social & hootsuite. (2021). *Digital 2021 Global Overview Report.*
https://wearesocial.com/blog/2021/01/digital-2021-the-latest-insights-into-the-state-of-digital

Winnicott, D. (2011a). *El hogar, nuestro punto de partida* [Home is where we start from] (A. Negrotto, N., Rosenblatt, & L. Wolfson, Trans.). Editorial Paidós. (Original work published 1986)

Winnicott, D. (2011b). *Los procesos de maduración y el ambiente facilitador* [The maturational processes and the facilitating environment] (J. Piatigorsky, Trans.). Editorial Paidós. (Original work published 1965)

Winnicott, D. (2015). *Realidad y juego* [Playing and reality] (F. Mazia, Trans.). Editorial Gedisa. (Original work published 1971)

World Health Organization. (2020, October 5). *Los servicios de salud mental se están viendo perturbados por la COVID-19 en la mayoría de los países* [COVID-19 disrupting mental health services in most countries] [Press release]. https://www.who.int/es/news/item/05-10-2020-covid-19-disrupting-mental-health-services-in-most-countries-who-survey

Yalom, I. (2015). *Psicoterapia existencial* [Existential psychotherapy] (2nd ed.; Diorki, Trans.). Editorial Herder. (Original work published 1980)

Zeidan, F., Martucci, K.T., Kraft, R. A., McHaffie, J. G., & Coghill, R. C. (2014). Neural correlates of mindfulness meditation-related anxiety relief. *Social Cognitive and Affective Neuroscience, 9*(6), 751–759.
https://doi.org/10.1093/scan/nst041

Zizek, S. (2020). Coronavirus es un golpe al capitalismo al estilo de "Kill Bill" y podría conducir a la reinvención del comunismo [Coronavirus is a blow to capitalism in the style of "Kill Bill" and could lead to the reinvention of communism]. In P. Amadeo (Ed.), *Sopa de Wuhan, pensamiento contemporáneo en tiempos de pandemia* [Wuhan soup, Contemporary thinking in times of pandemic] (pp. 21–28). ASPO.
https://www.perio.unlp.edu.ar/catedras/hdelconocimiento/wp-content/uploads/sites/129/2020/04/Sopa-de-Wuhan-ASPO_copy.pdf

Index

About the Authors

Marian Durao is an integrative psychotherapist, specialized in online therapy. She has a PhD in Psychology with a focus on Neurosciences, Cognitive and Systemic Psychology (University of Flores), a Master's degree in Emotional and Personality Disorders (University of Valencia), and is a researcher and postgraduate lecturer at the University of Flores. She is co-author of the books *Effective Treatments in Integrative Psychotherapy with Complex Patients* (2017) and *Online Psychotherapy: What It Is and How It Is Practiced* (2020).

Gaspar Segafredo is a psychotherapist with an existential and relational orientation and an undergraduate professor at University of Belgrano. He has a degree in Psychology (University of Belgrano), a degree in Journalistic Communication (Catholic University of Argentina), a Master's degree in International Relations (University of Bologna), and completed postgraduate studies in logotherapy and existential analysis. He is a therapist in the adult mental health service of the Ramón Carrillo Center (San Isidro, Buenos Aires) and a member of the editorial team of the *Revista Latinoamericana de Psicología Existencial, Un Enfoque Comprensivo del Ser* (ALPE).